LEADERSHIP
UNLOCKED

Harness the Power of Your Ambition
JESSE RHODES JR.

Leadership Unlocked: Harness the Power of Your Ambition by Jesse Rhodes Jr.

Copyright 2024 © Jesse Rhodes Jr.

ISBN: 978-1-7368209-9-5

All rights reserved.

Published by Vega Books. Vega Books is an imprint of Blue Cactus Press. We specialize in full service publishing for authors, artists, entrepreneurs, and service providers who seek to positively impact their communities. We produce high quality, market-ready books alongside collaborators from historically marginalized groups.

First edition. First Printing by Gray Dog Press in Spokane, WA.

Cover design and layout by Knic Pfost. Editing by Vega Books and Pinnacle Text.

Portions of the land acknowledgment used in this book, particularly text written in the Twulshootseed language, are from the Puyallup Tribal Language Program website. The mission of this program is, "to be kind, be helpful and be sharing in terms of revitalizing the Twulshootseed language by producing language users."

The Twulshootseed portion of the land acknowledgement translates to, "The descendants of the Puyallup Tribe lived on the lands along the shores of the Puget Sound. The tribe's people would make their homes near the water to harvest its abundance. The men would fish for salmon and other fish, while the women gathered clams, berries, and roots, and the elders told stories and taught the young people. The Puyallup people were known for their generosity."

We thank the Puyallup Tribal Language Program for the use of this valuable resource. Find out more about the Puyallup Tribal Language Program at puyalluptriballanguage.org.

Vega Books | caləɫali

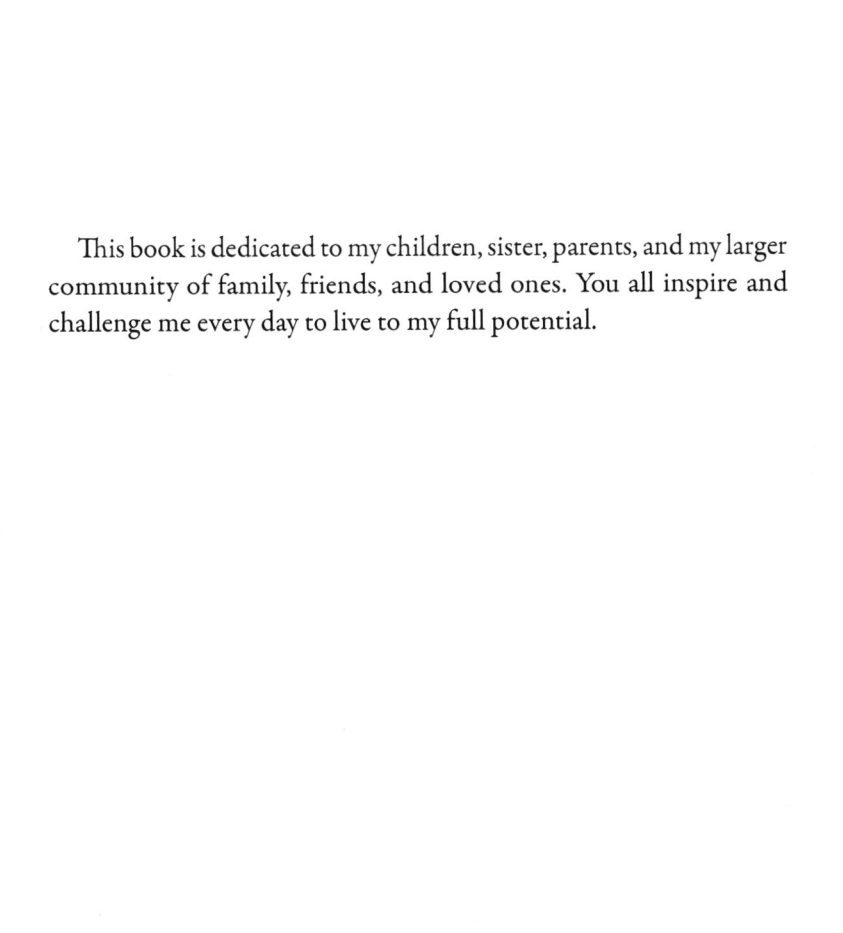

This book is dedicated to my children, sister, parents, and my larger community of family, friends, and loved ones. You all inspire and challenge me every day to live to my full potential.

contents

Introduction 9

PART I: PERSONAL DEVELOPMENT

Address Fear 21

   Fear, Poverty, & The Business of Books *by Christina Vega* 33

Cultivate Patience 45

Practice Gratitude 53

Build Endurance 63

   Building Endurance *by Philip "Sharp Skills" Jacobs* 74

Set Boundaries 79

PART II: RELATIONSHIP BUILDING

Nurture Trust 95

Listen 109

Gain & Provide Clarity 121

   Gaining Clarity & Building a Shared Vision at poco *by Jesse Rhodes Jr.* ... 127

Fulfill Commitments 131

   Living Life Inspired by Purpose *by Kaplan Mobray* 140

PART III: REALIZING YOUR FULL POTENTIAL

Inspire 147

   You Can Have Whatever You Want *by Amber Cabral* 154

Love 161

   Embracing Chiaroscuro by *Stephanie Ann Ball* 168

Acknowledgments 177

Index 181

About the Author 187

About the Contributors 189

Introduction

> "The greatest act of courage is to be and own all that you are. Without apology. Without excuses. Without any masks to cover the truth of who you really are."[1]
> — Debbie Ford

My mask is foolproof. I am a joyous, extroverted Virgo. I am also overwhelmingly positive, I love to laugh, and I am a true nurturer. I've been this way my whole life. I just love learning about people and listening to their stories. My magnetism to people of all backgrounds and walks of life has led me toward a life of leadership. I have been a leader in various communities for over twenty-five years, including academia, corporate America, affinity groups, nonprofit organizations, and family.

Underneath these layers of my personality, though, I sometimes struggle. I have trouble keeping up with my personal schedule and professional workload. And I often put my physical and emotional

---

[1] Ford, D. (2012). Courage: Overcoming Fear & Igniting Self-Confidence. Harper Collins.

needs last because I am too busy in "creator" or "giver" mode. It's easy for me to give all my energy away and forget to keep some for loved ones or myself. Because of this, the people closest to me complain that I am unavailable to them, emotionally and physically. When I am available, they tell me I'm always trying to "manage" them, as if they were my employees.

I'm not proud of it, but I have also lied, cheated, and stolen during my lifetime. The burden of those mistakes sometimes drags me back into the shadow of pain. When that happens, I imagine an energy vampire following me around every day, draining my joy and happiness until I'm hollowed out. The worst part is, when I imagine the energy vampire, I see myself. *I'm the vampire slowly drawing the lifeforce from my own veins and spitting it into the wind.* Gone. Wasted.

As painful as it is to share this with you, I knew I could not write this book without doing so. As a leader, it's important for me to acknowledge and share both the light and dark sides of my personality. How else can I inspire others, especially young leaders, to embrace their fullness and draw power from the array of their lived experiences? It takes balance, strength, and courage to present true portrayals of ourselves to those we live, work, and commune with. Opening ourselves to others permits them to do the same. Only then, with our emotional shields lowered, can we inspire each other and grow into our most realized selves as leaders. Removing those barriers produces limitless possibilities. It is through the removal of these barriers (which we often erect ourselves) that we unlock our leadership potential.

Over the years, I have wrestled with striking an emotional balance between the light and dark sides of my personality. I have come to love both my extroverted, energetic self alongside my tired, tender, and introverted self. I have come to tolerate the anger and suspicion that emerges when I'm depleted and the unquenchable enthusiasm I carry in my heart. I did not get here alone. And the road was not easy. It took decades of therapy, self-reflection, and boundary setting to recognize when my authentic personality traits morph into an ironclad mask of endless positivity and to stop or address unhealthy patterns as they rear their heads in my life. It took a lot of work to get where I am. And it was all necessary.

Why am I telling you all this? Because I've decided to change my narrative and take control of my life's story. I want you to see my transformation, as it happened, from the inside out. I also hope that by witnessing my transformation, you might see the possibility of that transformation sprout in yourself. May you embark on your own journey of lived, transformed leadership. I want you to harness *your* ambition and use it as a tool for shaping *your* leadership philosophy. Let that ambition drive you toward greatness. This is how we grow together.

To begin this journey, though, I first must share my story. My *real* and *whole* story. My messy and glorious story. I need to stand in my truth, unapologetically, so other leaders, particularly young and future leaders, can see themselves in me. Then perhaps they will begin to truly believe that no matter their mistakes, no matter their limitations, they are capable of almost anything within their lifetime, just like me.

I hope that entrepreneurs, business leaders, influencers, and community builders aiming for success, however they define it, will read this book and unlock a deeper understanding of how personal development can help you harness and direct your ambition toward self-actualizing your leadership potential. My own journey toward this understanding has been aided by mentors determined to pull me up alongside them as they meet metric after metric of success, often while I struggle to overcome obstacles I put in place before myself. Now, it is my turn to pause, look back, and clasp hands with young people eager to build remarkable things for our communities. It is with this intent that I ask you to sit down and listen to my story. Let my story connect with yours.

◇◇◇

I am unapologetically Black. I grew up in a Christian household in Philadelphia. I had a stable upbringing and parents who demonstrated the value of a strong work ethic. Overall, I was well-behaved in my youth, minding my parents and studying hard at school. I was often used as an example in my family of what a "well-adjusted" and "successful" young person looked like. I felt the weight and pressure of my family's expectations from a young age.

Still, I was no stranger to testing my parents' boundaries (though I was cautious enough not to transgress them too often). Crossing my parents led to swift and memorable punishment, and for good reason. For as long as I can remember, my parents worked two jobs each to support our family. They worked graveyard shifts in blue-collar positions. They didn't have the time, energy, or money to deal with me or my siblings' social misbehaviors. Knowing their capacity was low and the price for stepping out of line was high, I was not eager to be on the receiving end of their wrath. So, I learned how to avoid making my parents' (or anyone else's) lives harder than necessary. Doing so became my primary goal for many years. I learned to smile and laugh to please others, all the while tucking my true feelings away from the world. I constructed a mask, one I could use to conceal my genuine emotions from adults. Under my mask, I fawned my way into everyone's good graces.

It wasn't until high school that I deviated from this masking strategy. At the time, I got myself wrapped up in a verbal and physical fight with another young person. During the fight, they stabbed me. My injury was severe enough that I was hospitalized. Soon after, we were both forced to change schools. Our lives then went in dramatically different directions.

From what I know, the other student continued on a path of violence and turmoil. I picked myself up, put my smiling mask back on, and graduated from a strict Roman Catholic high school. Thanks to a teacher there who saw and nourished my love for data, I enrolled in a post-high school summer program offered by Drexel University to explore this interest further. The program was for Black and brown students interested in science, math, and engineering. By the end of the summer, I was hooked on data. That same year, 1993, I was accepted for undergraduate studies at Drexel University.

For the next five years, I lived on campus and attended classes at the LeBow College of Business. When I began my studies, I majored in Accounting. I worked hard to make my family proud, desperate to live up to their expectations surrounding education and career. I was acutely aware that I was the first in my immediate family to attend university and had the potential to be the first in my extended family to complete a five-year degree. I was fortunate that while attending the accounting program at LeBow, I received invaluable mentorship from an instructor. My instructor took the time to get to know me and how I think about the world. She talked to me about my challenges and successes in life. She also believed in my leadership potential, often encouraging me to lean into what was hard and what would propel me toward my expressed versions of success.

When I finally graduated from Drexel University in 1998 with a Bachelor of Science degree in Management Information Systems and Accounting and a minor in African American Studies, I was single-mindedly focused on beginning my professional career. I had spent the last five years listening to a familiar refrain about job searching: if you graduate from university, you will indeed find stable, if not lucrative, employment. But like many students of the millennial generation, when it came time to seek employment outside of academia, I didn't find that to be the case. Instead, I found that the strength of my relationships — both professional and personal — was just as integral to securing a position in a field related to my degree. I quickly realized how vital networking, making genuine connections, and finding community among peers and mentors in college would be to successfully getting a job.

Case in point: The individual who interviewed me for a position at an accounting firm after graduating from Drexel became one of the most impactful mentors of my early career. Her name is Debbie Hassan. Debbie interviewed me at Deloitte, a well-known accounting firm in Philadelphia, where I was eager to work. Deloitte is also one of the four largest accounting firms in the United States. Debbie was the hiring manager there. She was impressed by my GPA and resume, but she was more interested in my extracurricular activities.

You see, in addition to double majoring and working in the co-op program, I also co-founded the student chapter of the National Association of Black Accountants (NABA) and chartered the Alpha Chi Alpha Chapter of Phi Beta Sigma fraternity while attending Drexel. During my studies, I recognized a deep need to find belonging, be in community with, and share co-mentorship opportunities with other young Black professionals. If I was going to make it through college under all the pressure and workload I'd taken on, I needed to find a supportive community. I saw other students around me facing the same need. So, in 1994, while attending classes and working, I co-founded NABA, and in 1998, our fraternity charter was established. I hoped NABA and Phi Beta Sigma fraternity would become a place where I and others could find the community we needed to thrive.

It was around this same time, after graduating from Drexel and getting my foot in the door at Deloitte, that I learned something that shook me to my core. The individual who stabbed me in high school had been murdered during a drug-related incident. Even though I hadn't seen or heard from this person for more than six years, I somehow felt responsible for their death. Because of me, I thought, their life had been irrevocably changed. I — our fight — pushed them toward drugs, violence, and ultimately, an early death. I repeated this script to myself over and over again in the years that followed, punishing myself for a crime I did not cause or commit.

It took an incredible amount of support from friends and mentors, as well as a significant amount of personal development, to understand that this individual's death was neither my fault nor my burden to carry. I realized that the anger and hatred we had felt for each other in high school were simply reflections of our psyches projected onto each other. We were battling ourselves, not each other, raging against the parts of ourselves we didn't recognize or understand at that stage in our lives. Instead of working out our issues peacefully, we unleashed our violence on each other. Our internalized pain was externalized and then self-perpetuated. Now, thanks to the grace of God and the mentorship I received from my (very wise) mother, I can see that incident and the trauma it enacted on my mind and body with more clarity. I have forgiven us both, especially the teenagers we were then, for the harm we caused each other.

In time, I began to feel a desire to offer what I had learned from the violence of my youth to others. I started mentoring high school and college students as well as young professionals while working at Deloitte. I also remain a lifelong member of NABA, where I conduct community outreach and mentor young people seeking both professional and personal guidance. I have also served as the Advisory Board Chair at After School All Stars (ASAS) Puget Sound Chapter (Seattle) since 2019. ASAS is a non-profit organization that serves over 600 low-income, underserved youth in South King County and over 90,000 youth across the UnitedStates. In these and other mentorship experiences, I advise youth not to let adversity take them down a path of further disruption. I counsel them to focus on "The Five Ps of Personal Development," a term I coined to encapsulate the power of the following traits: patience, purpose, people, presence, and persistence.

These five value-based tools are what I utilized to excel in the interview that landed me my job with Deloitte. I took my time in the discussion, harnessing my patience. I focused on listening with a purpose, attempting to understand rather than be understood. I remained people-oriented and present to what was happening in front of me. I persisted in my efforts toward employment. I leveraged the strength of my relationship with my mentor, as well as the power of my connection to myself and my values, to achieve my goal of post-academic employment.

For a few years, my life continued like a modern-day fairy tale. I married my college sweetheart, we had our first child, Jason, and multiple promotions came down the line for me at Deloitte. Then, my second child, Jessica, graced our lives. To top it all off, my wife and I started a tutoring business that flourished in its early stages. On paper, my life looked and sounded like a dream for close to a decade.

Despite how peaceful it looked outside, unresolved relational issues also characterized this time in my life. I worked too much and traveled too often. I was not present enough at home to satisfy my wife's or children's requests for care. Then, after ten years of marriage, my wife and I began losing trust and respect for each other. Our communication deteriorated. We started working on our relationship, but we couldn't shape it into something that satisfied our needs, no matter how hard we tried. Adding salt to the wound, our mutual business began to show signs of a slow and sad decline. Finally, we could take no more. We closed our tutoring business, then divorced, and cut our losses.

Somehow, despite my strife, I had managed to excel at work. My natural gift for connecting with others and being solution-oriented helped me ascend the corporate ladder. I became the first in my family to make six figures. For someone who came from a blue-collar household and worked their way through college, this was a dream come true. Somewhat naively, I thought that if I could woo my corporate clients and leadership in the workplace, I should be able to win my wife and children back. Right?

Wrong. Well, it's mostly wrong. I did manage to win my family back, but my success was as short-lived as it was shortsighted. Neither my wife nor I was willing to put in the internal work required to change our habits or collaborate in good faith. But we had children together, and we wanted to make it work, as most parents do. So, I vowed to reduce my time at work, and my wife and I attended weekly counseling together. We began to think that if we got a fresh start in a new place, we could turn things around. To that end, after a short job hunt in 2012, I accepted a corporate position with Walmart in Arkansas. I moved ahead of our family, hoping to find housing and stabilize my new job. Then, my family would follow. My wife and I paused our counseling, thinking that we had more pressing things to focus on as the family prepared to reunite in Arkansas. But as quickly as we had returned to each other, my wife and I realized we could not bridge the emotional (and now literal) gulf that had opened between us. We agreed, again, to separate. My family did not join me in Arkansas.

Fast forward another decade, and now I find myself in Seattle. I live in a condo in a quiet suburb that overlooks Lake Washington and the downtown Seattle skyline. I am still learning to recognize and love myself without my mask. This personal development is not fun. At best, it is uncomfortable. But I prefer the discomfort to hiding my pain. I often feel alone, don't trust easily, and am bitter more often than I admit. And I have "failed" in business multiple times. I have also crafted a more authentic, peaceful, and prosperous life for myself. A true life includes people who love me and want to share in my burdens (even if they are inconvenient, uncomfortable, or ugly).

We must pursue personal development if we want to grow. Personal development has made me significantly more successful in life and relationships. I've noticed that the amount of time I put into personal accountability directly correlates to my ability to actualize my leadership potential. It has helped me land jobs in corporate environments at Walmart, Target, and, most recently, Amazon. These jobs have allowed me to travel the world. My work has pushed me to relocate from Philadelphia, Pennsylvania, to Bentonville, Arkansas, to Minneapolis, Minnesota, and now Seattle, Washington. My first flight (to Colorado) and international trip (to Neverlands) were with Deloitte. I will always treasure the excitement of that time in my career.

In all of my positions, I have faced innumerable professional challenges that demand consistent exercise and examination of the Five Ps of Personal Development, and which have pushed me to develop The Trust Model, a visual aid that encapsulates the necessary components of building trust as a pathway for inspiring ourselves and others. I dive into both of these concepts in later chapters of this book. Additionally, I've gathered "case studies" by various business professionals, entrepreneurs, artists, and writers in my network to emphasize learning points throughout the book.

I hope that by standing in my truth and offering the truths of others in my network, other aspiring leaders, particularly young, ambitious leaders, will see themselves in the content of this book. Then, perhaps they will begin to believe that no matter their mistakes or limitations, they can do almost anything within their lifetime. Assisting them along their journey is my highest calling as a leader.

Part 1

Personal Development

Chapter 1
Address Fear

> "In the course of history, there comes a time when humanity is called to shift to a new level of consciousness, to reach a higher moral ground. A time when we have to shed our fear and give hope to each other. That time is now."
> — Wangarī Maathai

When we do not know ourselves, our lack of understanding around our fears allows those fears to fester and grow. Over time, that fear will drive our behavior and we will be increasingly less likely to unearth the roots of those fears. They will fester in the dark, buried deep in our hearts. This is a defense mechanism our minds use to protect us from the unknown. Now, everyone's defenses look different. Mine show up as excessive positivity and humor. People who know me can see right through that mirage, though. They can feel it when I allow positivity and humor to build a wall between us, stifling a true and deep connection. This wall of positivity is my deflection. It allows me to skirt doing the important work of facing and understanding my fears, whatever they may be at that time.

Inevitably, though, I sit down and do the work of addressing my emotions and behaviors because I want to stand strong in my values and beliefs. And I want to understand myself. I ask myself,

What am I avoiding and why am I avoiding it?

What is this fear trying to tell me?

What am I afraid to find out about myself or others in a given situation?

What factual evidence do I have to support or negate this fear?

It's important to understand that behaviors based on fear keep us from acknowledging and acting on our most authentic, deeply rooted ambitions. Our fear keeps us stuck. Worse yet, when we are stuck long enough, we begin to allow the certainty of fear and mistrust to drive our actions. We create narratives based on our fears. And we judge others' actions according to them. Fear blocks us from seeing people and situations for what they truly are. We can only see the narrative we've created, and which we desperately want to believe. In this way, not knowing ourselves becomes a blockage to being in right relationship with ourselves and others.

We can end this cycle by thinking more critically about ourselves and the situation at hand. We can stop to consider that the way we see a situation may not be reality. Some situations might *feel* true to ourselves in that we perceive the situation to be a certain way, despite the facts telling us otherwise. But that truth may not extend beyond our individual experience. The trick is to step back from a situation and attempt to see it differently, from other people's perspectives. Doing so is strategic work. And we must out-strategize the fear that lives inside us. Only then can we see a situation for what it truly is.

One of the key elements of out-strategizing our fear is patience. Patience is allowing ourselves enough time to have an initial reaction to a challenging situation, then sitting with our fear, instead of running from it or getting angry with it, long enough to look at the situation more objectively. Patience allows us to outlast our initial, emotional reactions and make efforts toward considering new perspectives. *This must happen before we can begin to look for solutions.*

Recognizing and moving through our fear is a process, and it requires empathy, for ourselves and others. For those of us with children, we have plenty of opportunities to put this theory into practice. As parents, of course we want to care for our children, give them space to develop into well-rounded individuals, and, hopefully, inspire them to be their truest selves as they move through life. But we cannot do that without first cultivating a deep well of patience.

My opportunity to put this theory into practice came in 2022 when I sat down for a meal with my adult son, Jason. During the meal, Jason expressed that he felt stuck in his professional endeavors. He didn't know what to do, or how or when to "grow up." He wanted to explore his passions, but he couldn't see a clear path forward to do so. I offered him a reflection: Because he was so focused on not knowing what he wanted, he could not hear, see, or feel others trying to help him on his path in life. He especially couldn't see how his fear of the unknown was keeping him stagnant, both professionally and personally.

Now, let me backup a bit to give you more context. In January 2022, I acquired a restaurant named poco. poco (which is an acronym for Purposeful. Organic. Captivating. Optimistic.) was a restaurant and lounge in Seattle that I wanted to transform into a space where people could come together, celebrate, and be in community. Jason was looking for work around the same time I was opening poco to the public, and he mentioned he was interested in working with me there. Like any parent and business owner, I was delighted by the potential to be in a closer relationship with my son. I mean, my son wanted to work with me! And, I had the resources to make that desire a reality.

So, with an abundance of enthusiasm, I jumped into action. I gave my son the best position I could at poco despite his lack of experience in the restaurant industry, or as a leader in professional settings, generally. None of that mattered, or so I thought, because I believed in Jason. I could see his potential and I was ready to give him a chance. So I made him the new assistant manager of poco, complete with a team of front- and back-of-the-house staff, operational duties and responsibilities, and a salary to match.

Looking back, I see how my excitement, coupled with my impatience, led me to act against the best interests of Jason and poco. I *should* have been patient and asked Jason to tell me more about what he needed and wanted, and why he wanted to work at poco. But I wasn't. And I was too blinded by my desire to provide for my son to see that I'd made many assumptions about his goals and intentions. I'd assumed his goal was to rise to the top of the organization and step into leadership. I assumed he shared my drive to climb professional "ladders." And I didn't get curious and inquire about what working there meant to him. Instead, I jumped into action and strapped Jason with enough responsibility to immobilize him from the start.

Within only a few months of appointing Jason as the assistant manager of poco, Jason had closed himself off to the people around him and was not responding to requests for guidance and clarity. He became increasingly frozen with anxiety as time went on and as the pressure of responsibility weighed more heavily upon him. I didn't know it at the time, but I came to find out later that he was trying to hide the fact that he didn't know what to do. And he did not know how to ask for or accept help.

The impact of being closed-off like this, and of Jason's inaction, was an inefficient restaurant team burdened by fear. Jason's fear bred fear among the staff. As time went on, more and more people on his team were unwilling to make decisions unless those in higher leadership positions signed-off on them beforehand. And no one was willing to take responsibility for the outcomes.

Watching this play out in real-time, among staff and with my son, was excruciating. I knew I had to step in and be willing to have difficult conversations with everyone involved. That included facing my fear of confronting my son in a professional setting. It also included Jason facing his fear, which presented itself as imposter syndrome. Still, I knew that if I was going to step into conflict resolution with Jason and the staff regarding this issue, I had to move slowly and not rush the situation. I needed to be receptive to Jason's story and perspective;

remain open to what he had to say; be patient enough to hear his truths; and listen with the intent to understand, not fix.

From a broader business perspective, it's important to understand that if we can hold space like this — be receptive, patient, willing to understand, and not jump to action — we can demonstrate to others that we are ready and willing to receive people's truths. This is also how we cultivate vulnerability. And vulnerability begets more truth. In vulnerability, we name our fears, worries, hopes, and dreams. We allow others to see us without our emotional armor on, and vice versa. It is in this state of vulnerability that we can begin to understand the root of our fears and their associated challenges.

Ultimately, my advice to Jason was to be truthful with other people about not knowing how or when to move forward, despite his internal fear of doing so. What I didn't tell him was that after talking to him and listening to his perspective about coming onboard with poco, I saw more clearly the role I had played in instigating this challenge between him and the other staff. It was after hearing Jason's perspective that I realized I had saddled him with my own storylines about work and success, unbeknownst to myself. I acknowledged that by throwing Jason into a management position before he was ready to see himself in that role, I had thrown him into the deep end of a metaphorical pool without asking him if he knew how or wanted to swim. On top of that, I had expected him to manage people and build himself into my business under the same expectation I had placed on myself when I was younger: that of owning and managing a successful business, not just being a part of one. But Jason wasn't sure he wanted to do that.

Jason didn't see himself as a manager at that point in his life, let alone as the manager of a fast-paced, family-owned restaurant and bar in Seattle. Jason's version of success prioritized freedom and ease. As a parent and business owner, I had to accept that Jason's version of success, though it looked and felt completely different than my own, was valid.

My acceptance was essential to solving the problem at hand. I needed to accept that hiring Jason as a manager was akin to giving him *what I wanted*, not what he wanted. I had been blinded by my desire to recreate my own version of success, and driven by my fear that without me, Jason would not find his own way in this world. I didn't recognize the negative impact my hasty actions, personal desires, and fear were all having on my son.

Once I recognized Jason's desires, and my role in the situation, my next step was to acknowledge that I had internal work to do before I could address someone else's professional challenge. Sure, I could attempt to fix the situation at hand, but I had no business giving Jason professional advice until I conducted personal development. In this case, my internal work looked like examining my son's behavior and trying to understand his personal truths, then holding a mirror to myself and asking, *In what ways am I exhibiting the same behaviors in my life?* I knew that if I genuinely wanted to develop my leadership skills, I needed to answer this question.

> Leadership skills are in direct relationship to our self-awareness. When we couple self-awareness with a willingness to solve relational challenges, we exhibit leadership.

This holds true because when we engage with others, we reflect ourselves to and from each other. We become mirrors, seeing ourselves in others while they see themselves in us. So, instead of attempting to change someone's mind or lead them toward an outcome we desire, it's better to lay our cards on the table and tell them what we want. Then, we are more likely to accept that they will take what also works for them, and potentially, leave the rest.

We can only offer others opportunities, or pathways, on their journey through life. We cannot hold their hands and walk them along that path. Nor should we rescue them as they move through the world and deal with their own challenges. No one wants to move through life under the control of others, even if that control is gentle or well-meaning. Often, coercion and control are rooted in fear. And as we have learned, leaving fear unaddressed compounds relational issues.

Additionally, we cannot be present for every step of someone else's journey. If we were, it would become our journey. And we're not out to develop multiple versions of ourselves. That's not leadership.

> Leadership is offering someone guidance and support, then getting out of their way so they can make the best decision for *their* lives, not *ours*.

Anything more is a disruption of someone else's journey. We must trust that they know what is best for their life. Don't get me wrong. I want to nurture people in my life, especially my children, as much as anyone else. But if I, or others, overdo it, our support shape-shifts into control. We begin taking up so much space that we inhibit someone's ability to grow and develop. But if we get out of their way, they will likely rise to meet challenges in their own ways. This is where patience comes in.

We must have patience to allow things to unfold as the universe intends them to, in both our lives and in other people's lives. By allowing people the space they need to mentally and emotionally work through whatever they need to, we create opportunities for them to be independent and rise to their full potential. We also create opportunities for them to return to us of their own free will, open and looking for guidance. When and if they return, we must first listen to what they have to say. Give them time, attention, and patience. Then, only after we have taken in their views and information, should we offer our perspective.

We should also be direct and honest with people when we offer them our viewpoints. If we trust that they come to us for a reason and they are trying to instigate a change in their behavior, we will have better outcomes, and better relationships, with the people in our personal and professional lives. That change is not guaranteed, though, and it is not our job to ensure someone sees that change through. At this point, our role in the scenario is complete.

Now, let's return for a moment to the example with which we started, from the perspective I gained after speaking with Jason about what was happening at poco: My lack of listening and understanding of Jason's needs and desires led to his fear-based reaction of decision paralysis, which led to relational confusion at poco. I want to emphasize that my role, after confronting my role in the situation, and Jason's fear, was complete. I could offer solutions, but it was not my place to choose the right path forward for Jason or other staff members. My role in Jason's adult life is simply to balance sharing my perspective (when he asks for it) and giving him guidance based on his goals. My role is not to police his actions after our conversations or to make his decisions for him. I have to trust that even if I don't see it, our time together will affect his life's journey. We may never see or understand how we impact others. And we must make peace with that understanding.

> As leaders, we can make an impact without a show.

In the end, Jason decided his best plan of action was to step back from his role at poco. When he told me this, I was shocked, disappointed, and fearful about his future. But, once I let those feelings pass through me, I was able to sit back and listen to Jason's reasoning. And sure enough, after hearing his explanation, I could see that his desired course of action made the most sense for his life — even if it didn't make sense for mine.

Jason told me he needed to remove himself from poco because he didn't feel that managing a restaurant was his calling. Customer service and restaurant management roles did not inspire him. Instead of filling him with purpose and energy, his work at poco drained him and left him feeling inadequate and confused about his path. Worse yet, his role at the restaurant left him constantly feeling fearful of being exposed as an imposter. He couldn't picture his life as a manager in the long term, or imagine regularly pushing through the particular challenges that working in customer service requires one to address. Jason wanted to move his life in another direction, away from customer service or managing staff. He wasn't sure where he was headed, but he knew managing people was not for him.

When I heard him say those words, I was finally able to empathize with him. I too desire work that draws me in and feels congruent with my life's purpose. Knowing and following my life's purpose keeps me humble and grounded. Without that knowledge, I feel lost — which is exactly how Jason felt at that particular stage of his life. It became clear to both of us that what Jason needed most at this juncture in life was to find his purpose and let it push him forward. So, we parted ways professionally.

Now, several years later, after the dust has settled, I'm happy to say Jason has found work that resonates with him on a much deeper level. As Amber Cabral, a public speaker, writer, and inclusion and diversity consultant, reminded me in a podcast interview, "You have to figure out what inspires you to live your life to the fullest... Figure out what lights you up in life and business and hold onto that. Doing so will recharge you. And you need to recharge, especially when it comes to work."[2]

Today, my relationship with Jason is stronger than ever. Removing the stress of an intimate workplace relationship from our dynamic

---

2   Cabral, A. (2020, July 23). *Getting Un-Stuck*. Youtube. https://www.youtube.com/watch?v=Z4xcJto5NfA

was a positive change for us. Looking forward, I ponder how to bring the same level of intentionality and care to my other relationships, including those in professional, personal, familial, and creative spheres. Sometimes, my desire for intentionality plays out as me simply *asking* for that from someone and then waiting to receive an answer, regardless of how fearful I am of the potential outcome. Remember what I mentioned about putting my cards out on the table with Jason? This is the same principle. How things play out will be different in each case, but we can't let fear keep us from addressing what must be worked through. Addressing challenges and conflict might look like sharing a meal with someone and letting them know you want to talk. It may include a deep-dive conversation interlaced with elements of mentorship or concern. Or a walk through the park while holding hands and simply remaining silent as the other person works through a long-awaited response. In all cases, remember that moving through challenges takes time. It takes time to acknowledge, understand, and move through our fears and associated issues.

All we can do is keep moving through our fears and attempt to pour positive energy into other people and support them on their life's journey. Once we do that, we can sit back and wait to see if we sparked something within them. We must not let our fear stall us, or just as detrimentally, jump into action without pause for concern. That is runaway ambition. What we should do, instead, is move past our self-satisfying needs for immediate results and action.

key takeaways

- When we do not know ourselves, our lack of understanding around our fears allows those fears to fester and grow.

- Leadership skills are in direct relationship to our self-awareness. When we couple self-awareness with a willingness to solve relational challenges, we exhibit leadership.

- Leadership is offering someone guidance and support, then getting out of their way so they can make the best decision for *their* lives, not *ours*.

- As leaders, we can make an impact without a show.

transformative learning space

Consider what you read in this chapter and the key takeaways listed above. Write down a few ideas about how you can you apply these learning points to your own leadership practice. Include at least one actionable step you will take to unlock your leadership potential.

case study

Fear, Poverty, & The Business of Books
by Christina Vega

Christina Vega is the publisher and founder of Blue Cactus Press. They are also a writer, editor, and publishing consultant.

I'm afraid of being poor. And I'm afraid of failing at business. I'm especially afraid of my business taking the best years of my life away from my family and I, leaving me like an empty husk at a time in my life when I should be enjoying the fruits of my labors. These are learned fears that I gathered when I was a little kid. Back then, before I started school, I learned that my fear could make me invisible if I let it. My fear taught me to freeze whenever my parents started fighting (and they were always fighting). If I froze at just the right moment, their eyes would slide over me in their anger and find each other, or some other object, to terrorize. Meanwhile, I'd slink out of the house and avoid much of their chaos after returning to myself.

Throughout my childhood, my parents had aggressive, loud, and physically charged fights. They didn't hit each other, but they did everything else they could get away with to harm each other. Often, their fights ended with one of us kids or the neighbors calling the police. During their fights, they'd scream at each other, destroy photos and memorabilia, knock over bookcases, throw pots and pans, spray each other with water hoses, and once, even point a gun. My parents would weaponize whatever they could get their hands on or find the words for during a fight. Anything in their vicinity, including their kids, was fair game to them. So, from my earliest memories, I remember learning to sense their anger, pay attention to my building fear, and then freeze and disappear from their notice as soon as I could. This is how I remained safe as a child. If I was vigilant enough, I could become invisible long enough to slip out a window or down a hallway to the back door before they really got into it.

My fear helped me escape from a turbulent childhood, but as you'd expect, my pattern of freezing and disappearing followed me into adulthood and into relationships outside of my inner family. It has taken years of personal development, therapy, and literal stress response training from the U.S. Army to overcome my early, learned responses to fear. Sometimes, I still catch these stress responses embedded in my behaviors, even and especially in my professional life. In business, my fear presents itself as avoidance. I avoid hard conversations or truths.

Over the last year, I've come to realize that while my avoidance has kept me safe from some kinds of danger (anything that begins to look or feel similar to the dangers of my youth), it has also fueled counterproductive business strategies, decisions that undermine profitability, and a general over-commitment to people and projects for fear of conflict. My fear drives me to look away from these things, rather than examine them more closely. It keeps me from having to face the hard truths of my decisions, and to not question the possibility of subconscious motivations that negatively impact my business practices. My fear tells me that if I can avoid looking at my sore spots, I can avoid the discomfort of taking full responsibility for my actions. Clearly, my fear no longer benefits me, as it did in my youth. I want to tell it,

Thank you for keeping me safe all these years. But I don't need you to do that anymore. I can take it from here.

Because I can. And I'm eager to turn my personal and professional development up a notch. I want to bridge the gap between the business I want to build and that which I already have. But I can't do that without first addressing what is holding me back personally. I want to growth! I am the publisher and founder of a publishing company, Blue Cactus Press, which makes books that offer liberatory approaches to readers and hopefully, instigate positive social change in communities. My professional practice is also artistic. As a publisher and writer, I try to put words to parts of the human experience that otherwise, I don't have the language for or maybe can only point to otherwise. I believe that this naming of things is one of the first steps necessary to address them and the impact they have on our lives.

When this book is published, I'll have been in the publishing industry for eight years and running. Sometimes, I wonder what possessed me to bet on myself to the degree that I believe myself capable of building a business that could hold this kind of work. And build it from the ground up, as I have done over the years?

How the hell did I get my scared-ass self here, attempting work of this magnitude?

Then I remember my parents. Chaotic as they were, they were also serial entrepreneurs. My mother, in particular, instilled in me an incredible sense of self-assuredness that gave me enough confidence to give my dreams — any and all of them — a real shot. Why wouldn't I be able to accomplish something incredible when others have and routinely do? My mother was constantly encouraging me to do things I didn't think possible. She taught me to believe in myself. She taught me about positioning myself for success, how to make continual use of resources at my disposal, and how to push forward at all costs. Her lessons, and continued encouragement through adulthood, have carried me through the ups and downs of running a small business over the years. As a woman of color in the U.S., my mother has worked and fought for everything she's ever wanted or possessed in this life. She is no stranger to the alchemy of making something out of nothing. Her teachings about self-determination and hard work have carried me up and out of poverty, through college, into and out of the U.S. Army, and into a career of writing and publishing over the last decade.

Unfortunately, though, my mother taught me all this as a means of survival, not abundance. And most of her lessons were uncomfortable, to say the least. All those years of fighting with my father, and of scraping money together to make ends meet in our rural, poverty-stricken community on the outskirts of El Paso, Texas, meant my mother didn't have the luxury of softly or patiently teaching me how to move through this world. She taught me the lessons I needed to be successful in life while she herself was under constant emotional and economic duress.

We were poor. And we were always trying to climb out of poverty. I would say it was one of our primary pastimes as a family. My father was a long haul truck driver, by trade, and my mother worked while also caretaking, full time, for our family of six. We lived on rural, desert borderlands on the Texas, New Mexico, and the U.S./Mexico border, where money was tight for most people, regardless of which side of the border you lived on. Everyone lived paycheck to paycheck.

As a family, we were always on the brink of economic disaster. It seemed all my parents could do to keep us housed and fed. Obviously, living in this economic position didn't allow my mother the luxury of teaching me how to live from a place of being rested or resourced. Forget abundance and thriving, we were just trying to survive. Which meant my mother was always preoccupied and at her wit's end managing our precarious economic state. And she was always alone.

As a trucker, my father was more a voice on the end of a telephone line than a physical presence in our lives. When he was home, he and my mother mostly fought, were in an emotional hangover from fighting or were dealing with four rebellious kids. If they were unoccupied with any of those things, they ran businesses.

I learned my first lessons about business from my parents. Even though my father was always on the road, he still managed to turn his hobbies into businesses. More impressively, he'd convince my mother to do so alongside him. Soon after starting a business, my dad would quit his job and take on full-time duties at the new business. My mom provided operational support behind the scenes, often booking contracts and dispatching for my father. My parents shared a strong sense of serial entrepreneurship. Together, they ran an arcade, a butcher shop, a tow truck company, horse buying and selling, and car hauling businesses, to name just a few. But the money they earned — and they did earn a lot of money — was always dumped right back into their business. It never stayed in their hands long enough to make it home, so our family stayed poor even when business was good. Our money was always tied up or being paid to some contractor or service provider.

Now, I can see how this constant growth mindset led my parents, who didn't have a lot of resources to begin with, straight to burning out in their businesses. Constant growth relies on either large cash investments (which most people don't have) or a large and unsustainable energetic investment by those who work within the business. This strategy relies on an unending supply of labor, commitment, and energy. But as humans, we are not bottomless wells of labor, commitment, or energy. Our energy is finite and should be protected at all costs. Otherwise, we burn out. And our bodies may not necessarily return to their pre-burnout state. Our capacity for work changes as we age and grow and succeed and fail. We get tamped-down, or exhausted, by our practices over time.

Watching my parents start, build, and labor under their various business ventures while I was growing up made me realize that it doesn't take much to "lose it all," either. At the very least, it doesn't take much to lose it all under the "pull yourself up by the bootstraps," business mindset. Within the span of a few financially bad months, a promising business can easily go belly up. And it seemed to me that my family's businesses were always going belly up. Year after year, business after business, my parents cycled into and out of their status as "business owners." Each time, we'd land, as a family, back into poor living conditions. And each time, my parents' path forward seemed to come down to two drastically different routes: We could file bankruptcy and consign ourselves to using unreliable cars that never seemed to start and count our dollars at the grocery store each week until enough time had passed for us to be deemed worthy of "credit" by the bank; or we could pack up, leave our unpaid bills and half-formed businesses behind, and move to a new place to start all over again. If we were lucky, some of our bills would even disappear with the distance, new phone numbers, and unlisted addresses.

Of course, there were, and are, more choices for business owners to make when faced with the hard economic reality of closing down or changing the business model of an unprofitable business. But at the time, and with the hard economic truth of six mouths to feed and rent to pay, I only remember my parents ever considering those two options. Every time, my parents chose to pack up and move away over staying in place and facing the reality of their decisions (a.k.a. their failing businesses). So we'd move a few states away, spend some time getting back on our feet, and then slowly begin our long climb back out of poverty. My father would work a trucking job long enough to re-stabilize us while my mother worked odd jobs to cover our financial gap. But by the time we found our financial footing again, my parents would already be obsessed with another business idea. Inevitably, that new idea would turn into a business venture. And my parents would begin to shift our resources toward it. Like clockwork, my parents would begin to prioritize the success of their current business over that of our family. When the pressure got too high or either of my parents burned out from trying to "work harder," they'd get into a raging fight, abandon what they'd built, and pack up and move all over again. We were trapped in a repeating, self-fulfilling prophecy of economic instability.

It wasn't until our family landed in Chaparral, New Mexico, when I was in middle school, that my parents finally stopped starting over. They found a cheap plot of land with a small, single-wide trailer on it, and they decided to call it home. The trailer was not livable, of course. It only had two bedrooms (remember, we were a family of six) but that didn't stop them from trying to access a part of the American dream that had eluded them throughout their entire lives: home ownership. They managed to borrow enough money from my grandparents to put a down payment on the land, and just like that, they bought their first home.

It wasn't until after graduating from college with my undergraduate degree that my siblings and I learned my parents hadn't outrun anything in all those years of instability. Years of unpaid taxes had finally caught up with them. After we kids had all left home, my parents began a long and painful negotiation with the IRS. During that process, they somehow managed to hold onto the land, but they did end up paying all those taxes back.

Now, as an adult, I can see how I have carried the same practices and fears my parents held about money into my own professional practices. Like my parents, I am constantly afraid of falling into economic despair, and I tend to make decisions out of a survival-based mindset. But unlike my parents, I am more afraid of my life unraveling because of my poor business decisions than I am of simply being poor. I am just not willing to risk the wellbeing of my family on the promise of potential economic gain or a bygone dream of American prosperity. Still, knowing what I do not want to repeat has not been enough to keep it from pervading my practices. At the end of the day, I still don't know what it's like to not do business under constant economic strain. I don't know how to meet the needs of my business while also maintaining and prioritizing the needs of my family. I don't know how to operate from a mental state of abundance instead of scarcity.

This is why personal development is critical to my success as a business owner (and that of any business owner). In order to not just repeat the mistakes or poor practices of our past, we have to be willing to acknowledge the roots of those practices, examine how they have shown up in our current endeavors, and build a solid plan of action to move toward better outcomes. In my own life, this looks like facing my fears and biases surrounding money, class, and responsibility as they relate to me as a whole person, *not just a business owner*. I must become accountable to myself, first and foremost, and accept responsibility for my actions.

This is especially relevant now, as I face one of the biggest challenges of my professional career. Earlier this year, as winter gave way to spring, I realized that if I continue to run my publishing company as I have over the last eight years, without a change in my practices, I will run out of money within six months. When I realized this, my credit cards were already maxed-out and my bank accounts were draining fast. I had two staff members who depended on their paychecks as much as I depended on mine. The only way we could make it out of this mess, under my current practices and business model, was if one of our books became wildly successful and made it onto a national bestseller list. If that happened, I could use the money from the success of that book to bail myself out of the financial debt I'd accrued thus far. While this is actually, and surprisingly, a strategy large publishers use — banking on one title to make it to national bestseller lists and then using that success to cover the loss of other titles produced at the same time — it is not often used by small, independent publishers of my size and capacity. *Because it doesn't work unless you have money to burn.* And I've never had money to burn. More importantly, I knew this miracle was not something I could count on. Nothing, and no one, was coming to bail me out of the mess I was in.

The other, more viable option for moving forward with my business was for me to make immediate changes, at the foundational level, to my publishing practice, to see me through a transition period while I figured out a new business model. I would need to downsize my company to be able to operate with fewer or no additional staff and fewer resources than I wanted to. And I needed to do that responsibly, which included giving employees enough time and information to land new jobs and regain their own financial footing, as well. We all needed to salvage what we could. And I needed to maintain stability at home during the business's transition. To maintain stability, I would need to begin to prioritize the best interests of my family over the production of products or marketing events in all my business transactions. Every single time. This was hard, as I had been running my business much like my parents had: putting all my resources back into the business instead of taking them home to my family. I needed to believe that myself, and my family, are worth this prioritization.

In the end, I chose the option that prioritized my family's stability, and I chose to face the ugly truth of my financial decisions and how they got me to this crossroads. I decided not to close the business down and look for a new career. Instead, I took a hard look at how I was stewarding money coming into our business and how — and if — it was flowing back into my home and community in meaningful ways. I sat down and faced the reality of my balance sheets, profit and loss sheets, tax documents, spending habits, and problem-solving processes. I laid off my employees, giving them as much notice as I could. And I pushed past my embarrassment about "failing," about getting myself into this mess, and started asking for advice from my community members, friends, and family. I knew if I wanted to survive this lesson in life and business, I needed to resist my urge to hide the financial bind I was in from those

I care about. So, I started telling everyone around me what I was going through and inviting their feedback into the conversation. I needed to hear what other business owners and creatives had to say about the situation. *What would you do? How did you handle similar situations in your businesses? How do you advocate for your own financial wellbeing alongside the needs of the business? How do you cope with the economic stress of running a business?* I needed all the information I could get if I wanted to break my parents' cycle of running a business into the ground and dragging my family along with it.

I wanted to do things differently. So I committed to downsizing my publishing house, which included laying off employees, no longer hosting frequent (and expensive) events, and pausing our acquisition process. Moving forward, my strategy consisted of three main endeavors: I would prioritize the financial wellbeing of my family and my business (at its current size), fulfill my current financial commitments, and complete the creative projects I'd begun but had yet to wrap up. If I focused on those three objectives, I could get out from under the financial mess I'd created and hold my head up in business, instead of avoiding people and places for fear of confronting what had happened.

In the space that opened up since downsizing earlier this year, opportunities for building my professional practice as a workshop facilitator, consultant, and service provider have already appeared. To capitalize on these opportunities, though, I had to increase my self-belief. This meant spending more time in therapy and facing my longstanding fears, biases, and storylines. It meant spending a significant amount of time shadowing other professionals who were living examples of the kind of business people I wanted to become, or whose habits I wanted to adopt in my own practice. And it meant getting training and experience in my desired areas of expertise. Lastly, and most importantly, it meant I needed to spend more time at home with my family.

When this book is released, I will no doubt still be in the thick of this personal development and business transformation. I fully expect this path to be long and hard. What carries me through the work, though, is that my path forward is clearer to me now than it has ever been before. My work, at this stage of my life, is to learn to stay my course and sink deeper into the professional challenges I face, rather than avoid them out of fear or discomfort. I've come to realize that what I seek in business is more than financial stability (though that is still tantamount to my health and prosperity). I seek transformation. I seek liberation from the biases about business, money, and class that I learned as a child.

Chapter 2
Cultivate Patience

> "Maybe that's why life is so precious. No rewind or fast forward... just patience and faith."
> — Cristina Marrero

Philosophically, if we look closely enough at our work and our relationship to it, we can find ways to practice patience in almost everything we do. Practically speaking, having patience in our professional sphere can look like making time to meet with colleagues or direct reports, ensuring projects are completed despite challenges or setbacks, or allowing relationship-building to happen at a natural and non-rushed pace for everyone involved. Or, it might look like reconnecting with our individual purpose as it relates to our professional endeavors.

> Cultivating patience is not easy. It requires discipline, rigor, and commitment. But if we work to embody these values in our daily practice, we will positively impact our personal and professional relationships.

Over the last few years, I've been hard at work cultivating patience with myself, my family, and my business ventures. Each day, I attempt to move through my schedule with patience. I attempt to move slowly, not rush about. I practice taking time to hold space and energy for whatever presents itself to me on a given day. I use the word "practice" here because just like anyone else, I struggle to move with patience when my anxiety kicks in. My anxious-self wants immediate action. *Quick*, it says, *spring into action! You don't have time to think!* But I know this isn't the right move if I want to react in a more meaningful, thoughtful way. But when we practice patience, especially in our most anxious moments, we buy enough time to acknowledge the real — not perceived — situation at hand. The *real* situation is usually less dramatic and self-centered than we initially believe it to be.

> Patience buys us the time we need to clear our vision and see past our initial (emotional) reactions.

Once we move past our initial reaction, we can move forward with clarity and thoughtfulness. We can then troubleshoot challenges. In this way, pausing before we act cultivates patience. And that patience then allows us to harness our ambition until we are ready to take action.

At poco, not long after Jason left, I noticed staff facing daily challenges with patience. When they were frustrated with each other, and they often were, I could sense it as soon as I walked through the restaurant doors. As a leader and business owner, I could feel their anxiety against my skin like a scratchy, woolen sweater whenever I stepped into the space. They itched to implement changes and find solutions to longstanding problems we had yet to iron out. But they were doing so as individuals, rather than as a collective. And from what I could tell, with no underlying mutual trust.

In situations like this, I encourage people to resist the temptation to act. A better option is to take long, slow breaths to bring the body and mind back to a state of calm. This kind of self-regulation is an important preliminary step of problem-solving, even though most people don't practice it. Without this preliminary work, we won't be able to step outside of our singular point of view enough to consider that what's happening around us may be different than what is happening in our heads. This is not to say that we should dismiss how we feel. Rather, how we feel is just one data point out of countless data we have at our disposal. It is not the whole picture. There are always more data points to consider in a situation than simply how we feel or what we think as individuals.

When it came to understanding the mounting anxiety I saw among staff at poco, I knew my best strategy was to slow down, get myself to a place of calm while in the space, and observe staff while I was there. What I found beneath their general anxiety was a lack of team cohesion and an absence of group norms. On a hunch, I prompted some staff members to tell me about our organizational mission and vision at poco. But the staff members I talked to didn't know the mission or vision. There was no shared workplace culture at poco. From past corporate experiences, I understood that this was not because staff were uninterested in participating in workplace culture. More likely, it was because we — upper management — hadn't cultivated it yet! Somehow, despite my years of experience building and leading teams in corporate settings, I had skipped this critical step in team building at poco. Even though I objectively knew that establishing workplace norms and culture drives team cohesion, I had been moving so fast during our early, pre-opening phase that I completely forgot to cultivate workplace culture.

Now here we were, mired down in mutual anxiety and general mistrust. Anyone who walked through our doors could tell that there was unease among the staff. And that made it almost impossible for staff or patrons to relax in the space. Shame for my negligence as a leader and business owner clouded my mind. I wanted to run away and hide in a cave, but I knew I couldn't run from my emotions. Instead, I confronted them. I reckoned with my involvement (or lack thereof) in the situation. I spent a few days sitting with myself, journaling about what I'd noticed, what I'd forgotten to do in my haste, and who I might turn to for guidance. I started calling my trusted advisors and I sought their expertise. The more I acknowledged what I was dealing with and why, the clearer my mind became. The more I talked to others about what was going on, the more I was able to consider the situation from different angles. We didn't need a quick solution at poco, we needed team and culture building. We needed to recalibrate to a shared vision and do so in good faith with each other. We needed mutual respect and patience for the process.

Over the weeks that followed, the poco team came together and worked hard to build trust and respect among themselves. Staff showed patience with management (despite their earlier frustrations) by hearing management out and being present for the work of culture building. Management demonstrated patience by listening to grievances and requests. Management agreed to conduct training more regularly and be more present for daily problem-solving. We spent a significant amount of time talking about our organizational mission and vision. We acknowledged that in many of the previous cases of workplace challenges, tension was not related to the problem at hand. Instead, it was interpersonal tension that bubbled over into daily talks and challenges.

We agreed that our best path forward as a team began with a new process we'd first implement as individuals: pause, reflect, and address inner tension as individuals before we seek solutions to collective issues.

key takeaways

- Cultivating patience is not easy. It requires discipline, rigor, and commitment. But if we work to embody these values in our daily practice, we will positively impact our personal and professional relationships.

- Patience buys us the time we need to clear our vision and see past our initial (emotional) reactions. Then, with clarity and thoughtfulness, we can troubleshoot challenges. We can then develop a plan to move forward. Only then are we truly ready to take action.

transformative learning space

Consider what you read in this chapter and the key takeaways listed above. Write down a few ideas about how you can you apply these learning points to your own leadership practice. Include at least one actionable step you will take to unlock your leadership potential.

Chapter 3
Practice Gratitude

> "At times our own light goes out and is rekindled by a spark from another person. Each of us has cause to think with deep gratitude of those who have lighted the flame within us."
> — Albert Schweitzer

Accepting gratitude is akin to showing appreciation. When we accept gratitude, we are saying thank you to people in our network for participating in and supporting our endeavors. This requires us to remain open, or vulnerable, to people around us. "We have to be intentional about expressing gratitude," says Amber Cabral, "and we have to show people (through our behavior) and tell people (with our words) what we're grateful for. We can show people our gratitude by helping them with a professional challenge they're facing. If we help people, and we do so from a place of authenticity, we will strengthen our relationship with them."[3]

---

[3] Cabral, A. (2020, July 23). *Getting Un-Stuck* [Video]. Youtube. https://www.youtube.com/watch?v=Z4xcJto5NfA

On the other side of the same coin, accepting gratitude can also be hard work. When gratitude comes my way, I tend to throw it right back at the folks in my life who sent it along in the first place. It is incredibly hard for me to just sit with gratitude and rest in that feeling. Still, I understand that gratitude can be an affirmation.

If we allow ourselves to accept gratitude, we affirm that the effort we extended originally (and which brought that gratitude our way) was worthwhile. Our efforts had a positive effect on others. We can take it back even further to say that the intuition and/or impetus we acted on was correct. In this way, the more we accept gratitude, the more we affirm our intuition and decision-making. Being present enough to appreciate what we've created, and extending gratitude for those opportunities, builds the momentum we need to push ourselves toward fulfillment.

Cultivating gratitude is also a practice in relationship building. To show gratitude for what we receive from others, we must first be vulnerable enough to ask for what we need or want. We must be honest with ourselves about those needs and wants, and then articulate them to the people in our lives. In this way, our pursuit of gratitude is expanded to include our practices of self-reflection, honesty, vulnerability, and advocating for our needs.

◇◇◇

In 2013, after my divorce, I began making alimony payments to the mother of my children, who at the time, had become my ex-wife. I was financially strained but otherwise had begun to settle into a new phase in my post-marriage life. The pain and drama of my divorce had finally ebbed, and personal matters in my life began to take up less time and energy. As I reflected on my life at the time, I saw that I was taking care of my family, even though that care looked completely different than it had a few years prior. Where before I provided emotional support to my wife, I now provided financial support to my past partner. Before, she provided me with business savvy and encouragement. Now, I leaned on close friends and colleagues to bolster me when I needed it. Before, I provided food and shelter to my children. Now, I provide them with love, grace, support, and life guidance. In my reflection, I realized that being able to provide for my family in new ways was worth celebration. My life had changed drastically, and I had completed one phase of my life's journey and begun a new one. From that perspective, I could see all my family and I had accomplished together. I found self-belief in that moment, realizing I held the power to make significant adjustments in my life and come out alright on the other side. This realization was exactly what I needed to gather the courage and self-belief necessary to take another leap of faith. This time, I was ready to shift my focus toward my career and new ventures.

I wanted my career to help me add to the generational wealth my family had painstakingly worked for over the last few generations. To do that, I'd need to quit my job at the corporate offices of Target. I decided the best move for me was to temporarily return to Philadelphia, my hometown, as I prepared my finances and psyche for a move to Seattle. Once there, I would begin working as a corporate executive at Amazon.

My son and I agreed he'd come live with me in Philadelphia. In time, and if all went well, my daughter would follow. I was over the moon at the thought of being reunited with my children under one roof. I have always desired a close relationship with my children, so the opportunity to build and strengthen our relationship as adults by cohabitating with them motivated me more than any other factor related to this move.

Despite my initial enthusiasm, doubts crept into my mind. For two weeks, I questioned if I was making the right move. Would my children really be interested in living with me? Would I land in the right corporate role? Did I need to move to Philadelphia to tie up loose ends financially or was I just wasting money moving home and hearth to another city? And, what if I went through with all these changes only to learn my children didn't want to live with me? What if my new job was terrible? I spiraled into hypothetical nightmares about my future.

A week into crafting this personal echo chamber of doubt, I snapped back to the present. I was scared, sure, but hadn't I just proved to myself that I could handle change? That I know how to move through transitional phases and financial hardship? Didn't my son plan their moves while in Philadelphia with me? They had, I reminded myself. And this new entrepreneurial chapter of my life was something I longed for over the last decade, right? As I asked myself these questions, clarity came to me. I saw how easily my fear could hold me back from making the changes I desperately needed in my life.

I reassured myself of my intentions and abilities, and then I gathered the courage to move to Philadelphia. As planned, my son moved in with me. I was on my path, one that would eventually take me away from corporate America and toward entrepreneurship. I wasn't ready to quit my career yet, but I was building my exit strategy. I was securing a stronger financial future for myself and my family.

◇◇◇

Fast forward to 2022, on the evening of the grand re-opening of poco. Forty-four people came to our opening event. Of course, they all wanted to congratulate me. But I had sensory overload and wanted to squirm away from their well-wishes. When it came time for me to give a speech, though, I got on the stage and somehow, was able to be vulnerable with the people who had come to celebrate me, my family, and what we were building in our community in Seattle. I leaned into my discomfort in a way that I had never been able to accomplish before. I was able to give appreciation to people who had encouraged me to make this move toward entrepreneurship and receive encouragement and emotional support throughout the evening. I was able to remain present and accept their kindness with gratitude.

The evening felt organic. It flowed like water. I did my best to trust the processes and people I had put into place, and to know that conversations were happening with and around me for a reason. I was able to speak freely and unscripted. I minimized my perceived emotions of others and took their words and smiles at face value. The evening was easy.

By letting go of the veneer of control I and so many others cling to in our lives, I was able to witness just how many people were personally invested in me and in making poco a success. Staff were making it work right before my eyes. Was I nervous? Sure. But I was also excited to see the restaurant humming with activity. I recognized I had teams of people, between the restaurant, my family, and my community of friends and colleagues, who were dedicated to me and the successful fruition of my endeavors. I was overcome with gratitude for everyone's professionalism and teamwork that night. I couldn't have chased or manufactured a moment like this, so full of gratitude. The emotion I felt that night gave me energy as I engaged in a dance of receiving and sending gratitude into the world.

"You've inspired me," several people told me that evening. And even though I understood that more likely, I am simply the representation of *their* goals achieved, I was still joyous to symbolize our collective success. I am no stranger to people seeing themselves in me. They see my success as realized opportunities for someone they know, *someone just like them*. Each time someone celebrates my successes, I reflect the potential for their success. And when I receive that celebration with gratitude, we mutually reinforce the importance of moving toward our goals. We're also strengthening our intuition to take action, to step forward on our paths toward liberation. We inspire each other. And that is my higher purpose: to inspire others to follow their dreams and believe themselves capable of achieving them.

◇◇◇

Now, what happens if we don't hold proper space for receiving gratitude? We will erode our relationships and connections. And we may not get a second chance to make it right. When we cannot hold space for someone's gratitude or praise, we block them from energetically pouring into us. The moment we strive to inspire will be lost. Remember, inspiration and hope are delicate things. People take a leap of faith in coming to us. We are their emotional parachute. We must be present for their landing. We can't just let them fall. If we do, we will lose them. By being aware of this dynamic and holding people delicately, we nurture the growth of our relationships. Sometimes, this looks like the give-and-take of gratitude, and sometimes it looks like renegotiating an agreement or putting boundaries in place to protect ourselves.

> To the best of our abilities, we must hold space for people who move toward us with gratitude.

Of course, we can't meet every demand. And sometimes, there is energy at play that negatively impacts a situation, or which we interpret as being negative despite objective information to the contrary. When that is the case, we must tease that energy out and address it. But more on that later. For now, focus on the idea that if we remain open and in communication, we keep situations workable. Without open communication, we cannot positively contribute to a situation or person. If we are closed off, we put all the pressure of communicating onto someone else without telling them they must carry the load. Of course, we cannot know when these moments are coming. That is why the dance of pouring into others and receiving what they pour into us — or the dance of gratitude — is so important.

We are all climbing on an endless rope in life. As we approach knots above us, we face new challenges. For me, opening poco was a challenge. It felt out of reach, just beyond my comfort zone, and outside of my areas of expertise. But it also offered an opportunity I often long for, one in which I am fortunate enough to inspire others to reach up, pull themselves up alongside me, and climb even higher than I have. And ultimately, that is my higher purpose. I want people, especially the people around me, to climb up and over me. I want them to reach higher along life's rope than they ever dreamed possible. And to help others do the same. If I want to cultivate more moments like this, I must remain present and devote my attention to people seeking to engage with me with gratitude, and ultimately, love. We all must remain present in this way.

> For those who struggle with self-worth, know that we can still attempt to receive care and attention even if we don't feel like we deserve them. Doing so is not about us. It's about creating space for people to see themselves in what we are doing. This is how we inspire and lead others.

key takeaways

- To the best of our ability, we should hold space for people who move toward us with gratitude.

- Receiving care and attention — even if we don't feel like we deserve it — is important work. Doing so is not about us. It's about creating space for people to see themselves in what we are doing.

transformative learning space

Consider what you read in this chapter and the key takeaways listed above. Write down a few ideas about how you can you apply these learning points to your own leadership practice. Include at least one actionable step you will take to unlock your leadership potential.

Chapter 4
Build Endurance

> "The habits you have in times of challenge become
> the habits that push you in times of triumph."[4]
> — Kaplan Mobray

My mother once told me a journey of a thousand miles begins with just one step. I know she wasn't the first person to say it, but she was the first person to say it to me. And it was life-changing. While we are on Earth, the primary journey we experience is that of a short human life. We have less than a century to make our impact. And there is no destination. There is no end. Only a transition from one state of being to another. To be present for the entire experience, start to finish, requires mental endurance.

Paradoxically, we build that endurance by staying present to the needs of each day. How we greet each day matters. Each day, we must choose our first step, and choose it wisely. This helps us build endurance and keeps our focus on small, manageable patterns and behaviors. By doing so, we remove the weight, the burden, of our

---

4   Mobray, K. (2009). *The 10Ks of Personal Branding: Create a Better You.* iUniverse.

entire journey off our shoulders. We focus on one step, then the next, with the understanding that not everything will be rosy along the way. The challenges we face and overcome as we move from one day to the next will deepen our experience here on earth. We can learn to take the gratitude we collect along the way and let it refuel and restore us. In theory, we continue moving without distraction.

In reality, we do our best to acknowledge the past without falling into wistful reminiscence or bitter regret. Trust me, I can empathize with wallowing in the past. But if I can approach a new day with an open mind, stay curious about myself, and search for a bridge between my past and my present, I objectively know I will be better equipped for my present challenges. And if I can do this, so can you. Ask yourself,

Have I encountered this kind of challenge before?

If so, how can I handle it better this time?

What skills did I learn in the past that I can apply to my present?

Some of my most impactful internal work has happened in moments where I approach my past with curiosity and grace instead of criticism. "Stay present by being curious," Amber Cabral told me in a podcast interview once. "Curiosity is valuable…If you're present to the energy in the room, you have a good chance of seeing or hearing the lesson life is trying to impart to you in that moment."[5] In this way, being present in the day allows us to build endurance by redirecting our energy away from analyzing the past and toward problem-solving in the present. We take in new data points and leverage the information we gain to solve current issues. Deciding to continue each day on paths of curiosity, self-betterment, or leadership are ways we can practice endurance.

"When you have a mental game plan for change, you're ready for anything," says Kaplan Mobray in an interview recorded for the podcast, *Because We Are Home*. In his book, *The 10K's of Personal Branding*, Mobray says, "You have to be curious about the problem you are trying to solve. Simply knowing what that problem is will drive

---

[5] Cabral, A. (2020, July 23). *Getting Un-Stuck*. Youtube. https://www.youtube.com/watch?v=Z4xcJto5NfA

you to the solution you want."[6] I share similar beliefs to Mobray, who is an award-winning author, public speaker, and career consultant. Like Mobray, I believe our paths will deviate from what we and others expect. This is certain. But those deviations should be welcomed.

> When deviations from our path and purpose occur, we must let others pour their inspiration, love, and care into us. It is almost always in our best interest to receive this care.

In the care of others, we can find respite from our fears and gain information, knowledge, and insight we need but may not come across otherwise. In care, we find rest. And everyone needs rest. Rest allows us to recharge enough to return to our journey with a fresh mind and body.

> By taking rest when we need it, we build long-term endurance rather than succumbing to short-term burnout.

Accepting care reinforces the truth that we are not on this journey alone. There are almost always people helping us, whether we see or acknowledge that help or not. By receiving care, we create a healthy energetic ecosystem of giving and receiving. This applies to humankind, the land we walk on, and the plants and animals we interact with. By

---

6   Mobray, K. (2009). *The 10Ks of Personal Branding: Create a Better You*. iUniverse.

giving and receiving, we assist in moderating Earth's natural rhythms, and in keeping our own rhythms in sync with them. We must operate in agreement and connection with each other. Sometimes this is as simple as making a cup of coffee for a loved one in the morning, or as complicated as accepting financial help to purchase a home and build stability for our children.

Understanding how we operate in our ecosystems helps us stay humble. Humility is freeing. When we remain humble, we can more easily stay on our daily path, putting one foot in front of the other, because we have surrendered to the idea that greater forces are at play in our life and may impact us in ways that alter the direction we take on our larger journey. Humility provides ambition with longevity.

> We are not guaranteed to achieve our goals. We are not even guaranteed to accomplish our daily work. We sure as hell are not guaranteed to get what we want. The only thing that is guaranteed is right now.

If you are able to accomplish what you set out to do, consider yourself blessed. Because at any moment in life, we may face new struggles and challenges that force us along uncharted paths. Being humble means appreciating that we are free and able to walk our path while facing reasonable struggles. Surrendering to struggle builds our mental endurance. This is how humility and endurance are linked. By leaning into both, we gain perspective on our positionality and privilege on this earth, which then lifts the weight and stress of our larger journey off our shoulders once again.

Don't get me wrong; you get a say. As Amber Cabral reminded me in a podcast interview, "You don't have to live the life you've been told to. The life you live might not be the life you thought you would live. You might not be faced with the choices you wanted to face. And it might take you longer to get where you want to be than you thought it would. But you still get a choice. Ask yourself, what do I want my life to look like?"[7]

> Look to those people in our lives who exemplify endurance and humility, and you will unearth moments of agency and choice.

It is especially important to look to people who operate within a larger energetic ecosystem than we typically do on a day-to-day level. Most likely, these are people who do community work, engage in local or regional governance, and/or are activists, care workers, or public servants at any level — from serving a family at home to a worldwide ambassador. Find those people in your life and look to them for guidance.

My mother and father are also people who exemplify endurance in all they do. In their marriage, I see the power of embodying endurance and remaining committed to cultivating a healthy relational dynamic. My parents have been married for fifty-four years now, and each year, I see them capitalize on the benefits of their long-term, stable relationship. They know each other so well they can navigate hard times with nuance, empathy, and care. Individually, they have given me some of the most impactful advice of my life, especially when I've been faced with adversity. My father, who is a veteran of the Vietnam war, has

---

[7] Cabral, A. (2020, July 23). *Getting Un-Stuck* [Video]. YouTube. https://www.youtube.com/watch?v=Z4xcJto5NfA

taught me that no matter how hard things are in life, we can endure. We are subject to something more in this life, and we should not let our daily trials and tribulations distract us from our higher purpose. My father's endurance is rooted in this belief.

My mother approaches endurance from another angle. She is an empath. She is a strong example of someone who continuously pours love into others, and who allows that love to drive her toward success. Over the course of my life's journey, she has provided me with constant encouragement. In every memory I have of her, I can feel her pride in me. I see how she has held me up so others can celebrate my accomplishments alongside her. When I receive her care, I am filled with a desire to live up to her admiration for me; I want to be the best version of myself. Her energy makes me feel unstoppable. It fuels me when I feel lost and unsure of myself. It makes me want to push harder to achieve my goals and help others alongside me to do the same. I almost always end up rerouting the energy she pours into me into my children and loved ones.

At every significant juncture in my life, including going to college, becoming an accountant, and betting on myself as an entrepreneur, she has been at my side. She saw greatness in me each time, even and especially during my most troubling times, such as my divorce from the mother of my children. When I have been in physical and emotional pain, she has been a shoulder to lean on. We limped forward together. She told me, "You will wake up one day and feel your greatness, too." She reminds me that each step on my path, no matter how hard, has a purpose.

My mother has a strong sense of self and incredible faith in her personal beliefs. Yet, she does not try to convince or control others to believe the same things she does. More often than not, she lets go of the idea of control. By letting go, she remains present and in rhythm with the energetic flow around her, shifting as situations require. This surrender and fluidity are the basis of my entire life view. I strive to remain present each day, noticing small moments of challenge and success, beauty in the mundane, and honesty and transparency in social interactions. I am present because I watched her remain present. I am authentic because she remained authentic.

Through my mother, I learned we cannot skip steps in or quicken our journey. If we attempt to do that, we will miss the lessons life is trying to teach us. My mother sees the importance of moving slowly and intentionally. She knows that we have to enmesh ourselves in our challenges as deeply as we do our celebrations. We must settle into discomfort to build endurance. She once told me she hoped these lessons would help me expand and grow. That is the parent in her. It is also the parent I actively work to cultivate in myself. I try to take the lessons she gave me and impart them to my son, while also giving him the space he needs to work through them on his own. Even if I think I know what he needs, I can only offer my advice and then step back.

Watching, observing, and learning how he sees the world helps me identify areas I need to grow in. Parenting is truly the best example of the reciprocal nature of allowing energy to pour into and out of ourselves and those we hold close. In this way, and many others, parenting is leadership. By giving our children space to create and take ownership of their life's journey, we cultivate inspiration. Inspiration and ownership lead to the delivery of our promises. If we are overbearing parents and push our ideas onto our children without stopping to consider how they move through the world on their own, we erode any self-accountability budding within them. The more we allow our children to take their own steps, the more we encourage their accountability and empowerment. Not doing so will stifle them and prevent them from learning their own lessons. Offer children unconditional love, support, and direction without engineering their path to self-growth. This is perhaps one of the most impactful lessons my mother taught me. I must trust that how my children live their lives will be better for them than what I could imagine for them. Only they know the rhythms of their heart.

There is an undeniable connection between parenting and endurance. Parenting creates and stewards new life. The first stage of parenting is sparking life and taking responsibility for it. The second stage is protecting life and learning how to truly be there for our children. Then, we move into a phase in which we can see and appreciate our children as separate from ourselves. We see them as their own people.

Perhaps the most terrifying stage of parenting is letting them fly. In this phase, you will have doubts. *Did I prepare them to fly? Did I give them an accurate instruction manual? Where will they land? Can they navigate once they get there?* Understandably, the separation and uncertainty in this stage is hard for most parents and children. Some children, even as adults, will stay in our nest. Some will fly away immediately, never looking back. But if we look within ourselves and take stock of how we have been pouring and receiving energy to and from our children, we will find that we have prepared for moments like this. We have been monitoring their journey and responding to their needs all along. We are in the midst of a lifelong practice of building endurance. As parents, we are perpetually moving along parallel paths with our children.

This is where vulnerability comes in handy. When we are vulnerable, we are transparent about our desires and fears. When we are transparent, we allow others to see our true selves, and give them courage and impetus to pour into that chasm inside us that we've laid bare. We allow them to contribute to our understanding of what's happening around us. If we are vulnerable and transparent enough to allow our loved ones to see our uncertainty about our parenting, they can help us step back, gain perspective, and see the truth: We are not and have never been in control of our children's lives. We can see that the time for surrender is always *now*. Our children must walk their own paths.

Many of the lessons and perspectives I've picked up along my journey through life point back to remaining open to energetic in-and-out-pourings. It bears repeating that we must build emotional endurance to remain open and true to ourselves. If we do this, we can become a positive example to others about what life can look like. My lived experiences paint a picture for other people to scrutinize and draw from, especially my children. I am important only as an example to them and others. I must remain humble enough to see my life experiences and former pathways as potential options for others to take. Sure, my outcomes carry insight others can draw from, but the pathways I leave open behind me are just as important as the outcomes. I want people to see themselves in me, to empathize with my mistakes and successes enough to galvanize pathways that may be opening within them. I want them to believe that whatever they are about to attempt is possible. This is empowerment. This is what my mother offered me, what I offer to my children, and what I hope to offer others.

key takeaways

- When deviations from our path and purpose occur, we must let others pour their inspiration, love, and care into us. It is almost always in our best interest to receive this care.

- By taking rest when we need it, we build long-term endurance rather than succumbing to short-term burnout.

- We are not guaranteed to achieve our goals. We are not even guaranteed to accomplish our daily work. We sure as hell are not guaranteed to get what we want. The only thing that is guaranteed is right now.

- Look to those people in our lives who exemplify endurance and humility, and you will unearth moments of agency and choice.

transformative learning space

Consider what you read in this chapter and the key takeaways listed above. Write down a few ideas about how you can you apply these learning points to your own leadership practice. Include at least one actionable step you will take to unlock your leadership potential.

case study

Building Endurance
by Philip "Sharp Skills" Jacobs

Philip "Sharp Skills" Jacobs is a hip-hop artist, author, consultant, entrepreneur, and founder and owner of Rebel Firm, LLC.

When I think of what endurance means to me, I think of a runner continuing to race even when they're physically tired, emotionally spent, and the world is telling them to quit. A runner with endurance will keep running. No matter what. They have grit. And usually, they've trained hard for those exact moments when every cell in their body is ready to stop. That's true endurance.

An experience that truly tested my endurance occurred in 2021. At the time, I was going through a terrible divorce and rediscovering myself as a single man in a high-profile professional position. I was the executive director of a startup organization where I interfaced with some of the most powerful CEOs in the country. I was also a newly single dad with two energetic boys aged nine and six.

To keep my life running smoothly, I had to perform at an incredibly high level in all aspects. Still, I unintentionally bumped heads with the person I reported to at work. For the sake of this story, let's call this person Marissa. Marissa wasn't keen on giving second chances or much grace to those who reported to her. So, it didn't come as a big surprise that shortly after we butted heads, she decided not to renew my contract as executive director of the organization.

Now, I had only been in the role of executive director for about seven months. And I was in the middle of an incredibly hostile divorce that cost me thousands of dollars a month in attorney fees. (Keep reading and I'll tell you how much I spent before the divorce was final.). Luckily, Marissa had enough decency to give me a few months' notice before she kicked me out the door completely. She also offered me a lesser role at the organization, but I wasn't feeling it. Instead of taking the lesser role, I decided to take my chances and look for work elsewhere, even though I didn't know where or what that work would be.

I decided to use that interim time to figure out my next professional move. At the time, I was still in the thick of battling with my ex-wife for 50/50 custody of our sons. More than anything else happening at the time, this personal fight to stay in my sons' lives was taking a deep emotional and financial toll on me. It was during this time that I had a major choice to make. One of my options was to quit my job hunt for something significantly better and accept a lesser role at the same organization. If I did this, most likely, I would lose the ability to pay for lawyer fees and subsequently, lose access to my sons. My other option was to keep going, to keep running, which in this case meant enduring a significant career pivot and aligning my personal life to my new goals.

As I weighed my options, I looked at my sons sleeping peacefully at night, safely under my roof. I knew I had to keep running. In order to do that, though, I would have to conduct a personal, internal inventory. I wrote out all the things I had going for me, in detail, and where I wanted to go in life. I focused my attention on those things, and only those things, each and every day. I also needed to stop thinking about what I *feared* could happen. This combination of focus and release empowered me to push beyond my limits and keep my eyes on what I prized most: my sons and the life I was building with them.

I want to share exactly what I did to endure this period of my life so that you can see what my endurance looked like. And maybe, you'll use it as a template for building your own endurance. Here are the things that helped me get through this tumultuous time in my life:

Every day, I prayed, read my bible, and spent time worshiping God. My faith was my bedrock.

I went to the gym consistently and worked on my physical wellbeing.

I hired a personal MMA trainer who I still train with at least three times a month.

I hired a personal fitness trainer who I still workout with at least three times a month.

I found a great therapist who I still meet with once a month.

I worked on my music and released an album. Did I mention that I'm a successful hip-hop artist under the name "Sharp Skills?"

I wrote a book called *Elephant in the Room*: *A business parable about race and equity conversations in the workplace.*

I went to church regularly.

I became a personal development junkie. I kept my favorite motivational speakers on repeat on YouTube.

I got serious about saving and investing my money and learned how to become better at both.

I read a lot of books.

I focused on my sons and had as much fun as I could with them.

I worked on my business, Rebel Firm, LLC.

I spent more time with friends and family who genuinely love me.

I dated women who celebrated my successes and allowed me space to focus on my priorities.

I started taking better care of myself overall and gave myself permission to enjoy physical pleasures like getting regular manicures, pedicures, and massages.

All of these things helped me to step into a better life for myself, and my sons, while simultaneously getting me through the darkest period of my life to date. Each of these habits became my water source, enabling me to keep running my race in life. I even remember joking one day with my personal fitness trainer about how I couldn't accept Marissa's offer for the lesser position because I had bigger muscles now. I knew I could do better. We both got a good laugh out of that one because it was partially true — psychologically and physically. The thing about endurance is that the longer you exercise it, the more confidence it breeds.

After close to a year of doing the work of improving myself holistically, I began seeing results in several areas of my life. Each time I saw and felt the results of my endurance, my confidence grew. This confidence was the currency I needed to put a down payment on a better life. I created great habits that I stuck to, and which I still have to this very day. Several years later, I'm still actively practicing my faith, working out, going to therapy, spending time and having fun with loved ones, working on my business, releasing books and music, and much more. The endurance I developed through that dark time in my life sharpened my consistency. I've been reaping the benefits ever since. That $40,000 I spent in divorce attorney fees has since been recouped by what feels like a tenfold increase, and not solely a financial increase.

As of October 2023, I'm preparing for the launch of my first board game, my fifth book, and my seventh album. I'm also dating an incredible woman and have great relationships with my sons. I'm more successful in my business (earning more money and notoriety) than I have ever been in my entire life. I'm living proof that if you push past the voices and circumstances telling you to quit your race, you will emerge victorious. And you will be able to help other people, those who feel like throwing in the towel, with your story, just like I am with mine.

Chapter 5
Set Boundaries

> "Boundaries give us the space to do the work of loving ourselves. They might be, actually, the first and fundamental expression of self-love. They also give us the space to love and witness others as they are, even those that have hurt us."
> — Prentis Hemphill

Boundaries are not intrinsically "good" or "bad." They are simply a means of honoring our limits and engaging in self-love. Setting boundaries, both for ourselves and for others, allows us to connect and engage more authentically with each other. Only when we set boundaries can we see and feel each other's core values and bring to light potential barriers that may keep us from living in alignment with them. If we do not take the time to align with our core values or our inner truth, we will never be able to support ourselves. And if we cannot support ourselves, how can we possibly support others? Instead, we must do the inner work necessary to support our truest, most authentic selves. We begin that process with self-examination. Ask yourself,

What are my truest, deepest desires surrounding my purpose, potential, and identity?

What life experiences are my truest desires rooted in?

What barriers keep me from acting on my truest desires?

What is one step I can take to self-actualize those desires?

If we think of our truest desires as values and beliefs already rooted within us, we can remove the pressure of "starting" on brand new paths or completely rearranging our lives to get to them. Of course, there is work to be done to evaluate which of those desires we want to act on or allow to shape who we are in the world. We may find some of those desires, values, and beliefs to be things that took root within us when we were young, passed-down from generations before us. Sometimes, we find desires that slipped through cracks in our psyche's fence, perhaps when we were not living with intention or were trying new ways of being. In these cases, it's best to acknowledge, hold, and release those desires from the necessity of action.

When we identify desires that reflect and reinforce our most actualized self, we can begin the work of preparing ourselves to carry out our higher purpose, regardless of what it is. We must ask ourselves what steps we can take to live in better alignment with those desires. Better yet, what is the next, singular step that we can take today to align with and/or act on those values?

Oftentimes, we allow ourselves to be distracted from this work. Or we refuse to look closely at what is motivating our actions or ambition for fear of what we'll learn about ourselves. Instead of addressing our past, we jump into new relationships, jobs, vices, or hobbies. We bounce from one thing to another. Our attention is everywhere all at once.

> While it may be satisfying at first, in the long run, flitting from one thing to the next leads to passive compromises that bring us no closer to living our truths.

We are too busy ignoring our needs and refusing to look inward to identify and act upon that which will propel us forward in life. We cannot let short-term desires drive our behavior. Instead, we must construct boundaries around our behavior that will help us realign with our deepest, true desires. When we speak and behave with boundaries, we construct maps that show ourselves and others how we want to be treated. Boundaries are just one of many tools we need to engage in self-healing along our life journey.

We must also engage in recognizing and releasing our burdens. As humans, we are quick to blame ourselves for how things work out in our lives, especially when conditions are less than ideal. When we are dissatisfied, when situations don't pan out as expected, or when things take a turn for the worse, we are more than happy to heap shame, humiliation, and self-doubt on our backs. Despite how this first appears (and feels), we must admit that this is, at least in part, our ego expanding to cover our pain. We blame ourselves, victimize ourselves, and then fall apart instead of picking ourselves up off the floor and troubleshooting what actually happened. We get caught up focusing on surface-level circumstances and then refuse to examine underlying causes. When we are too invested in our personal success like this, we cannot move past our own involvement in less-than-ideal circumstances. In this way, we allow ourselves to be distracted by our wallowing. This is often true for both small, daily interactions, and larger, more impactful life events.

If we hold onto all these ego-driven narratives (a.k.a. our expectations), we will get stuck. Of course, we always have expectations, whether we acknowledge them or not. The possibility of not meeting those expectations often creates a deep-rooted fear within us. As we collect these fears and carry them with us through the world, they become burdens. Unfortunately, we tend to hide these burdens from people in our lives. We get it in our heads that we must carry the load silently, as if this protects our loved ones or ourselves from the implications of our fears. And we often refuse to release those burdens and let ourselves rest. "Stuck is a state of mind that cannot exist without complicity," Amber Cabral reminded me in a conversation about career and personal development recently. "To be stuck is a choice. To get unstuck, take action."[8] As easy as that sounds, I understand that sometimes, we are not as ready to step into our deeper truths as we sometimes think we are.

> We create the very limitations that hold us back in life. This is why self-reflection is so important. By self-reflecting and looking inward to discover the origin of our fears, we gain an understanding of ourselves that can serve as a roadmap for future decision-making.

Through the understanding made possible by introspection, we shed light on that which we are most terrified to confront. When we take a long and clear look at the origins of our fears, we can reduce

---

8   Cabral, A. (2020, July 23). *Getting Un-Stuck*. YouTube. https://www.youtube.com/watch?v=Z4xcJto5NfA

the anxiety and stress surrounding them. We can then use this newfound self-knowledge to combat not only our personal fears but the debilitating fear of the unknown.

> Self-reflection helps us retrieve the power we infused into our fears and redirect it toward higher purposes in our lives. This is how we can get out of our own way long enough to listen to, understand, and inspire others to do the same.

Consider when I used to lead projects while working in corporate America. Every time I started a new project, I believed, erroneously, that I had to "solve it all." I placed the burden of solving all our challenges on my own back! When others resisted my approach or didn't get onboard with my plans, I would repeat myself over and over, thinking maybe if I explained things differently, someone would finally "get it." I alone held the solution, or so I believed. In reality, I was the one who was not "getting it." I was too wrapped up in my head about solving problems according to solutions I had already decided were the correct courses of action. I couldn't see past my own ideas enough to listen to what others were telling me. I was limiting myself to only a single set of ideas and information. Not only was I impeding my own success, I was impeding everyone else's as well.

This also held true in my romantic relationships. When I was with long-term partners, I would focus on what I was missing in our relationship rather than the beauty of what I had right in front of me. I shackled my partners with fulfilling all of my needs and wants in a relationship, reducing them to what they lacked and what I wanted, rather than what they brought to our relationship and what they wanted. This left my partners feeling belittled and disempowered.

It wasn't until I received feedback at work that I realized that my behavior was stymying myself and those around me. My leadership team pulled me to the side one day to deliver feedback from their ranks, and from an individual who I'd left feeling powerless and "less than." They sat me down and explained how my behaviors were impacting others at work, as well as loved ones at home. My need to prove myself *to myself* and insanely carry the weight of achieving everything, overcoming all challenges, at any expense, was my limiting belief. I was crushing my own success.

I began a journey of self-reflection. I scheduled time to myself on my calendar to sit and think, to journal, to self-reflect. I wrote about situations in which my expectations weren't met; how I felt; how others reacted; final outcomes… It became increasingly clear how this limiting belief was affecting other aspects of my life. I realized that what I thought were simply my personality quirks – not being comfortable in new spaces and trying to steer situations toward my desired outcomes despite resistance – were actually fears in disguise. I was afraid of not being or doing enough. Somewhere along my life journey, I picked up the idea that I must earn my comfort. There is a voice inside my head that says I must work, perform, pay a pittance, etc., before I can even begin to find comfort, rest, or relaxation. And I sure as hell can't ask for help. I am not worthy of help, so I will do it all myself despite the outcome.

Because of this deeply rooted (and erroneous) fear, I get lost in my head every time I go somewhere new. Being "in my head" keeps me from being present in new spaces. I perform expected behavior: laugh, keep things light, be personable. People will like me *and will believe I am enough* if I can prove my worth by performing for them. I will script entire experiences in my mind and act according to my expectations instead of being present, vulnerable, and open enough to receive someone's outpourings. It is safe. I can be with people while maintaining emotional distance and then push forward through the experience, and life, at a breakneck speed.

Looking back, the experience of buying my first home and rental property, respectively, also reinforced that I have a repeating pattern of acting on my fears instead of pushing through to act on my long-term desires. When I purchased my first rental property, I didn't tell my parents about it. More truthfully, this was the second real estate purchase I had kept hidden from them. Purchasing a home is often the most significant and expensive purchase a U.S.-based consumer will make in their lifetime.[9] I was moving fast, as always, and avoiding conversations with my family. If I avoided their conversations (I suppose we can call those conversations accountability) I could avoid examining my own motivations for purchasing the properties. I was keeping a safe emotional distance from people I knew could break me open like a coconut and draw the answers out of me.

But by keeping my family in the dark (via inaction), I was unintentionally excluding them from my life. And for what? So I didn't have to be accountable to myself or anyone else? Deep down, I knew my fears (*What would they say?*) and my ego (*I'm not accountable to anyone. I'm grown!*) had teamed up and were running the show.

When I finally opened up to my family, something unexpected happened. They relished the opportunity to be so intimately involved in my life! They weren't judgmental, they were incredibly supportive. They encouraged me to continue to prioritize financial decisions that could change the trajectory of my and my children's futures. They were also eager to celebrate me as I overcame such monumental financial milestones as home buying and investing in property. Through their outpourings, I realized they had gone through something similar when I was young. They had lived this before and understood how the pressure, challenges, and risks of purchasing property could weigh someone down unless they had done enough internal work necessary

---

9   Knueven, L. (2019, August 15). The 7 most expensive things you'll ever pay for, according to financial planners. *Business Insider*. https://www.businessinsider.com/personal-finance/most-expensive-things-americans-will-pay-for-2019-8

to stand in all that uncertainty. They knew how impactful acknowledging that burden could be, let alone celebrating it.

By allowing my folks to celebrate and connect with me, to celebrate what I had accomplished, I was allowing myself to live in the present more fully. I was able to stop thinking about the next day and the next month, stop worrying about the year to come, and simply enjoy the moment at hand. I finally stopped carrying the burden of worrying about the future. And when I was finally able to be present with my family, I was able to acknowledge and express my gratitude to them.

Writing this book is another example of self-examination as a tool for self-discovery, re-alignment with desires, and boundary setting. I don't expect everyone reading this to go out and write their own book. But they might be willing to take on a daily habit of journaling or they'll research what it takes to craft a book or look into storytelling as a new hobby. Each of those actions could lead them to take another step along their own life's journey.

Practices like this, which encourage reflection, can become powerful tools of self-discovery. Through journaling and art, we carve space for our inner voice to sing our unspoken stories onto the page. By acknowledging those stories, we give them power. We shed light on the deepest parts of ourselves which we usually keep locked inside. We remove the power from fear of the unknown and anxiety surrounding "being seen." We can use these artistic practices to create containers to hold our examinations of our behaviors and desires. We create boundaries for self-reflection.

Self-reflection is a continuous practice. We won't arrive at a finish line and we'll never be "done" with this work. Rather, we reach milestones or reflection points in our lives, and if we're able to, we re-orient our lives to match our intentions. This should be a continuous exercise for our minds. And just like any muscle, if we stop working our mind, it will atrophy. This is why it is so important to keep inspecting, appreciating, and building on our personal development.

Conversely, if we refuse to do this inner work, we will not be able to live in the now, nor engage with others, because we are blindly looking to and worrying about the future or reliving our past over and over again. In both cases, most likely, we get stuck worrying about what people will say and do if they knew what we were truly feeling. We can't engage in conversation if information is only flowing in one direction: toward us. To truly be in conversation, we must be present enough to actively listen to people and engage with them in response. We need to gain clarity on what they are saying and understand what core values drive their behavior. This is how we meet people where they're at. We cannot support someone if we don't understand where they're coming from, don't listen to their stories, or empathize with their lived experiences. If we haven't done the work of self-examination, we will never be able to put our fears aside long enough to fully engage with who or whatever is in front of us. Learning to be present, to listen, to be engaged, and to empathize with others makes those we interact with feel seen and heard. And that is all people really want. They want to feel *seen*. I'm talking about feeling *deeply seen,* as in way down deep on a cellular level.

We demonstrate that we see people's authentic selves by building trust in our interactions with them. Every time we make an effort to remain present enough in an interaction to listen and understand the information being relayed to us, we build trust. People take chances when getting to know each other by testing the safety of shared interactions. They start by offering relatively safe information and waiting to see how we respond. If we listen and respond positively, they may open up and give us more intimate information about themselves. If we do not, we send a signal that we offer no safety for their vulnerability or honesty in our interactions. If we respond positively to their information and demonstrate that we see and hear them, they will begin to believe we can hold space for them. Communication becomes a trust exercise and a demonstration of respect. As people feel our respect and begin to trust that we can remain present with them, they will continue to open up. Trust compounds. And the quality of our relationships increases as trust increases.

Once we have learned to be present and demonstrate trust with people, we can learn to support them, relate to them, and accept them where they're at. Now, we often think of supporting someone as going to great measures to help them at the expense of our own time, energy, and resources. But offering support without boundaries will leave us depleted. And we cannot support others if we cannot support ourselves. This is why boundaries are pivotal in our relationships. Instead of giving endlessly, we must learn to give what we can in a moment, then step back to let those we're supporting seize what we've laid before them and run with it.

Sometimes, support is as simple as allowing someone to be themself, their whole self, and encouraging them to achieve their goals (not your own idea of what is good for them). If we are lucky, they might voice their boundaries, too. Now, remember when we said boundaries are like roadmaps?

> Consider someone's boundaries as a roadmap to loving and supporting them. Understanding their boundaries gives us valuable insight into how to engage and disengage with them.

Boundaries inform us about how and when to create distance in a relationship without assigning or taking on blame. Respecting boundaries, both ours and others', might mean letting go of people, businesses, relationships, or love when our intuition is coupled with data gained from being present in interactions. I like to think of intuition as a muscle that needs to be exercised and strengthened by use. It helps us discern, without words, whether an opportunity will have a positive or negative effect on our lives. Tap into your intuition by asking yourself, *does this serve me and my higher purpose?* If the answer is no, move forward and away from that situation with as much grace and respect as you can. This will free you.

If you do not heed the answer laid before you, you will degrade your connection to your deepest-rooted desires and beliefs. Undermining that connection is another way of avoiding the inner work necessary to facilitate clear communication and boundary-setting with others. When we refuse to do this work, we end up carrying our baggage with us from one place, person, or relationship to the next.

The formula for boundary setting begins with self-inquiry. Pay attention to what you discover about yourself. This facilitates self-realization. Allow that self-realization to bind you to the present moment. Listen to the information flowing into you right then and use it to gain clarity on who or what is before you. Use that clarity to set and uphold boundaries. Then move through the world with intention. This is how you step into your higher purpose.

key takeaways

- While it may be satisfying at first, flitting from one thing to the next leads to passive compromises that bring us no closer to living our truths in the long run.

- We create the very limitations that hold us back in life. This is why self-reflection is so important. By self-reflecting and looking inward to discover the origin of our fears, we gain an understanding of ourselves.

- Self-reflection helps us retrieve the power we infused into our fears and redirect it toward our higher purpose in life. This is how we get out of our own way long enough to listen to, understand, and inspire others to do the same.

- Consider someone's boundaries as a roadmap to loving and supporting them. Understanding their boundaries gives us valuable insight into how to engage and disengage with people.

transformative learning space

Consider what you read in this chapter and the key takeaways listed above. Write down a few ideas about how you can you apply these learning points to your own leadership practice. Include at least one actionable step you will take to unlock your leadership potential.

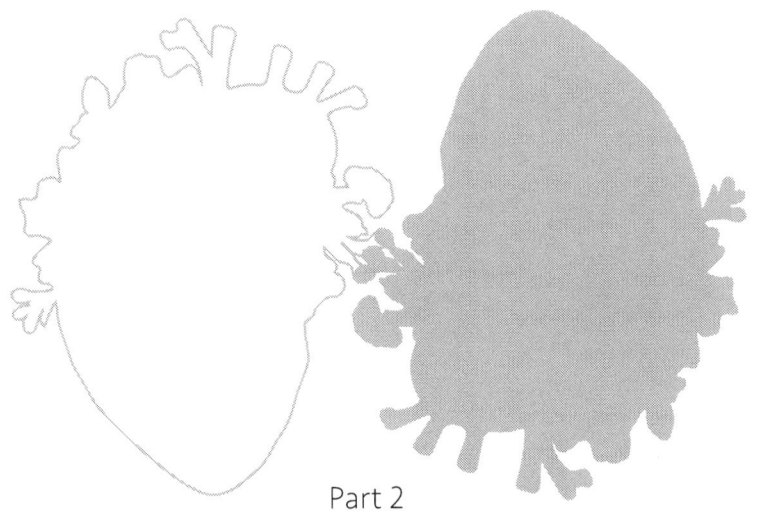

Part 2
Relationship Building

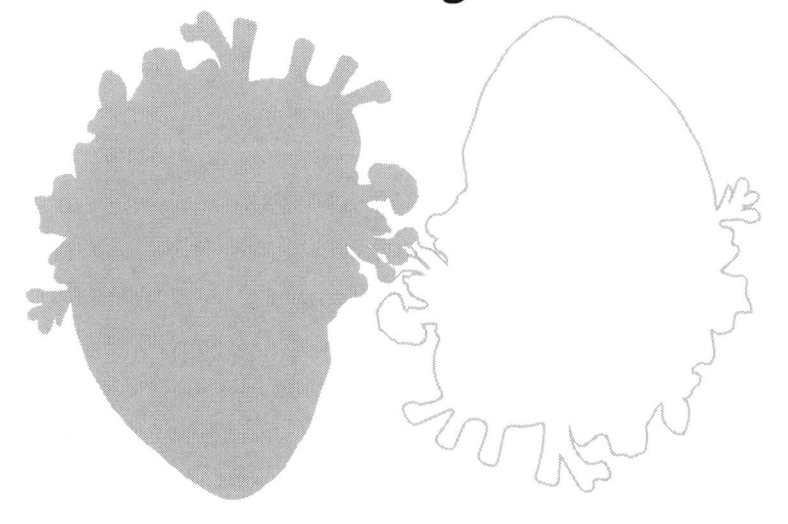

Chapter 6
Nurture Trust

> "Trust and truth are intimate companions,
> but we must also acknowledge that
> there are many kinds of truth."
> — Esther Perel

We cannot inspire others without first building mutual trust with them. This trust, and what we do with it, is incredibly important to our position — in career, community, and family — as a leader. When we lead, we must trust others enough to give them the space to explore and be creative in life. If we do, we will end up with far better outcomes for everyone involved than if we had not. Most likely, we will move in a different direction than we initially expected. If we remain flexible and open to new ideas, especially from those we share space with, we will be rewarded with stronger ideas, deeper relationships, and more brain power as we work through challenges and triumphs.

It might be tempting to only seek information from close peers or folks from our inner circle, but to limit ourselves to information coming from those with whom we share values, ideas, or experiences is to severely limit our potential for success. We should strive to remain open to information from peers, as well as direct reports, bosses, coaches, colleagues, children, partners, friends, and family. Doing so is challenging, but it is absolutely a worthwhile endeavor. We should aim to become practiced at receiving feedback and information, whether it be critical, counter-intuitive, or from perspectives that differ from ours. As diversity, equity, inclusion, and anti-racism practitioner Krista Peréz often says in her consulting practice, "We must not let feedback startle us."[10] Otherwise, we will miss out on valuable information that could very well push us toward growth. Everyone we come across in life has something to teach us. This is why trust is absolutely necessary for our growth as individuals and leaders.

> When we trust people, we can cultivate space within our conversations for information to land with a foundation of mutual respect and good faith.

With a foundation of trust, suddenly, we can find solutions to problems, come up with great ideas, rise to new challenges, or implement plans that otherwise might have remained hidden from us. Our trust in others is a demonstration of our willingness to find a favorable path forward without insisting on controlling the journey.

Early in my career at a large organization, I was asked to conduct a risk assessment for moving away from manual processes and human involvement. I had just started working there, and I didn't know much about the company or the workplace culture. But I wanted to prove myself to my team, so I proposed an idea that was out of the norm.

---

10   Peréz, K. (2022). *Unearthing Our Roots: Restorative Practices for Cultivating Spaces of Belonging*. Blue Cactus Press.

I suggested we hire out a section of our workload to a vendor. My proposal was accepted and I excitedly put a team together.

When my team began our work, I sat all the teammates down and told them about my vision for the project: to plan and execute a risk assessment for the organization's financial processes and controls. Now, the traditional approach to new projects like this in the corporate world is to conduct an initial risk assessment, audit the project, write a report in support of implementation, and finally, implement the project. But I wanted to take an agile approach (a project management approach that dissects projects into sections and encourages continuous innovation within each section). An agile approach is iterative, meaning whatever you're working on gets better and better as the project continues because you've been improving it with each new version of the workflow. Our agile approach involved the team spending as much time as possible on assessment, followed by getting feedback from focus groups, making recommendations, and then repeating the entire process as necessary.

Over three days of ongoing training, I brought our team together and tried to gain their trust. I used vision boards, I explained how and why my approach would work, and I gathered supporters for my line of thinking. People were nervous and I could tell they didn't trust me or my vision yet. I can't blame them, as I had been at the company for less than six months. Moreover, the organization had a very reactive workplace culture. Team members innovated by problem-solving rather than by taking proactive steps to get in front of a problem before it even happened. They were rewarded for fixing problems instead of preventing them. The approach I suggested — an agile approach to discovering preventative controls — is counter to that culture. If implemented, my plan would have us moving against the existing work culture.

Despite being met with heavy resistance from company leadership, my team rose to the challenge. We started with theory, thinking and discussing how we wanted to do things differently. Then, we brainstormed favorable outcomes. We carried out our work slowly, building entirely new processes for how to go about our work together before we even got to the work itself. We spent a significant amount of time developing our game plan, assigning each other responsibilities, talking about shared visions of success, and agreeing on underlying conceptual frameworks. Once we got to the work itself, we had to learn to recognize, measure, and implement changes without the initial inputs that a reactive culture handed to us on a platter. We built our controls upfront, as opposed to problem-solving later. We built an entirely new and collaborative foundation for our team within this single project.

Our team also became painfully aware of our growth points. We couldn't hear my boss when he talked about his version of success. Instead, we only heard his criticism about our methods. When my boss spoke, we were hypercritical of his word choices and tone. We got hung up on his criticisms, hurt that he could not see the incredible amount of energy we were pouring into our work. In hindsight, I believe we reacted this way because we did not have the necessary trust underlying our collaborative space to enter conversations with my boss in good faith. Philosopher and writer Conner Bouchard-Roberts defines good faith as, "a commitment to the truth of the underlying statement." Consequently, we couldn't focus on anything other than our emotional reaction to his words. *We kept getting startled by my boss's feedback.* And no one, including my boss and those on my team, was willing to move toward a collective version of success (though I'm sure several paths could have led us there).

Don't get me wrong. My boss was not particularly hard to work with or unreasonable. There were moments in our work together when he offered an olive branch to the team. Several times, my boss mentioned that our team would do well to implement monthly business reviews to ensure we were all moving toward the same goals on the same path. Now, this is a basic and known necessity that most project managers implement on a weekly, monthly, or annual basis. But in our haste to carve a new path for ourselves within the organization, our team let our monthly business review meetings fall to the wayside. We did not heed my boss's advice, though my intuition suggested we were making a mistake by ignoring valuable insight. Instead, the team focused on completing our daily work and pushing forward to formalize our agile approach. We believed doing so would be enough to keep us all on track. Unsurprisingly, that was not the case.

Without check-ins, teammates began using different language to describe what they were doing. We started confusing each other, making assumptions, and building off work we individually created for our own part in the project. When we came together, we spent a significant amount of time untangling our language. Without our monthly review meetings, we weren't doing the work of establishing shared language within our project. Nor were we updating my boss with the information he needed to take to his leadership team and advocate for resources.

This lack of information (due to a lack of trust), coupled with confusion around shared language (due to poor listening), compounded to create a shoddy relational foundation with my boss. It caused a palpable lack of clarity regarding where we each stood with each other and what we were collectively trying to accomplish. The team could see and feel my boss's lack of faith in our ability to complete our project with the requested deliverables. He needed us to do so with data and reports that put our work into perspective along with the overarching vision of success at our organization. To achieve that, we needed to address underlying cultural aspects of workplace dynamics that were at odds with our agile approach. If we couldn't address and shift the expectations toward the process instead of the outcome on a given project — if we couldn't convince people to address the root of a problem instead of developing a band-aid solution to it — then it didn't matter what our team achieved. Leadership would not be able to see past our initial refusal to align with their methodology. They would not trust us to complete our project and propose necessary improvements because their expectations were for something different.

> We cannot deliver successful outcomes to stakeholders if their expectations are for something completely different than what we present to them. If expectations are different, we must have enough trust built up between all stakeholders to bridge the gap between their, and our, expectations.

My team and leadership were out of alignment with each other. Still, the team carried on courageously. I suspect some of my team members could tell I was starting to lose hope that the project was going to work out for us. Getting ready to go to work began to feel like stepping onto a battlefield. But our work felt foundational to my own growth, and we were in too deep with this project to start all over again. I struggled to keep from falling back into my old way of thinking and doing things, which was to entrench myself even deeper into doing things "my way" when met with resistance.

In the end, what my team and I built together was inspirational. We (eventually) learned to trust and depend on each other. We managed to cobble together a common language, or lexicon, to ensure accuracy and clarity in our work. We talked about shared values, goals, and approaches to work in a workplace culture that usually didn't allow for that type of relational work. We even identified what we believed held the organization back and the workplace trauma that we knew needed to be addressed before a deeper level of organizational success could occur.

When I reflect on the full experience of that project, I see that a deeper sense of mutual trust would have led us to better outcomes. Each time we moved forward without enough underlying trust in each other, we reinforced communication barriers that kept us from achieving collective success. We had to learn to trust each other and not let fear direct our actions. We learned to listen more attentively to each other. We got clearer in our communication. And we learned to allow space for people to approach their work from a foundation of lived experience, rather than relying solely on data, academics, theory, or external expectations for a stated outcome. We had to trust that everyone was mutually invested in our collective success and would prioritize it over individual achievements.

Recommitting to team success and deprioritizing individual achievement in the interest of collective success were two of the biggest leadership development challenges we faced during this work. I learned to put my ego-driven work (of changing the organizational problem-solving approach) down. This dramatically changed our working dynamic because my team could finally trust that I was in the work with them, not above it, and that I was not obsessed with driving my own objectives forward. I also learned to trust that my team was inspired and committed enough to deliver us to the finish line. They just needed enough space to do so on their terms. I needed to believe their work was as impactful as mine, and that they were as committed to the work as I was. Anything less was patronizing at best, and disrespectful, at worst.

Once I finally laid down my desire to prove a new methodology would be beneficial to this project, I was able to redirect my energy to strengthening trust within our team. I leaned into the discomfort of abandoning my vision to make space for the magic of what others could bring to the table. I cultivated trust by being present with and earnestly listening to my team members. I started telling them aloud that I trusted and valued them. They needed to hear words of encouragement and see me demonstrate trust through my actions at work. This was humbling work for me, but it was integral to my growth as a leader. The old me would have gotten bogged down in the fear of not being able to perform, or of not delivering the target if it was not to my own satisfaction. But the new me, the version of me willing to check my ego, push back where appropriate, and then hold faith in what my team could accomplish, moved with trust.

This experience, and the leaders who guided me through it, were pivotal in helping me understand the importance of aligning expectations before delivery to stakeholders. This became the foundation of my signature Trust Model, which shows us how active listening, clarity, and commitment are the building blocks of trust, which makes space for true inspiration.

The Trust Model

With the Trust Model, I demonstrate how active listening is the first and most necessary ingredient in the trust-building journey. Active listening includes listening with the purpose of understanding, rather than being understood. When we employ active listening, we gain clarity about the wants and needs of each party involved. Active listening and clarity build off each other in a beautiful, reciprocal cycle. Together, these two inputs set the relational stage necessary for commitment and trust to flourish. When we are committed to one another or a project, we can better uphold any mutual agreements involved. Fulfilling those agreements is perhaps one of the most powerful foundations for building trust that we can offer others, as it is a demonstration of our words in action. Once we have all three of these building blocks — active listening, clarity, and commitment — we can truly inspire each other. With inspiration, we deliver outcomes that create new pathways and lift others along the way. Here is a visual representation of the Trust Model.

TRUST BUILDING INPUTS

ACTIVE LISTENING
Listen with purpose and the intent to understand rather than be understood

CLARITY
Gain clarity about the wants and needs of each party

COMMITMENT
Validate words with action and remain committed to expressed agreements

OUTCOME

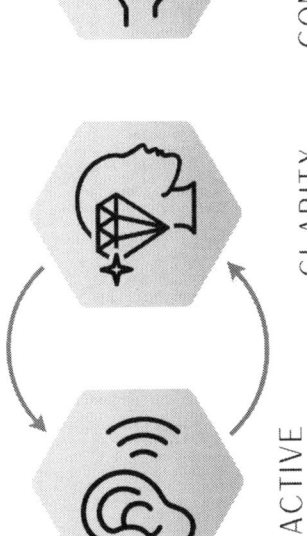

INSPIRATION
Deliver outcomes that create new pathways and lift others up along the way

Nurture Trust | 103

In addition to galvanizing my ideas about what it takes to build trust and inspire others, I also learned about Situational Leadership®11. Situational Leadership® is the idea that we, as leaders, look at the task at hand and what it requires, then tailor our leadership style and actions to what our team members need to accomplish it. Situational Leadership® is getting in sync with teammates about the level of effort and communication needed to accomplish something. It is engaging earnestly with people, not overshadowing or refusing to engage with them unless we can do so on our own terms.

Situational Leadership® is also boundary-setting. A boundary can be a roadmap, a clarification, or a set of operating procedures within our relationships. Boundaries allow folks to understand how best to relate to each other and build operating norms that work for those within a project or challenge. Boundaries take us out of our heads (and the narratives we build there which may not be true) and put us back into effective engagement and communication. Boundaries help us cordon our ambition and orient it toward places where it is needed most.

My experience leading a team to accomplish the Agile Risk Assessment added a wonderful richness to my time at that corporation, even though I could not recognize it at the time. During the situation, I was too exhausted to see how that position and project expanded my leadership and communication skill sets. In retrospect, it was one of the best projects I've ever been a part of. As a team, we were faced with numerous challenges, and we couldn't help but learn as we jumped over each hurdle. I learned that diversity within a team, and the lived experiences and perspectives of those within it, are integral to any team's success. This was one of the most culturally, racially, and geographically diverse teams I've ever been a part of. As a group, we learned the power of trust-building, clarity, and listening. In the end, our final report landed harder with our leadership team than any of us could have anticipated. Our report, and the product, were some of the

---

11   Situational Leadership is a registered trademark of Leadership Studies, Inc. dba The Center for Leadership Studies.

best work I've coordinated to this day. Many of the people involved were able to see that trust matters, especially when going up against established workplace culture.

key takeaways

- When we trust people, we cultivate space within our communication for information to land with a foundation of mutual respect and good faith.

- We cannot deliver successful outcomes to stakeholders if their expectations are different than ours. If expectations are different, we must have enough trust built up between all stakeholders to bridge the gap between their, and our, expectations.

- The Trust Model shows us that active listening, clarity, and commitment are the building blocks of trust. When all three building blocks are present, we are better able to inspire others.

transformative learning space

Consider what you read in this chapter and the key takeaways listed above. Write down a few ideas about how you can you apply these learning points to your own leadership practice. Include at least one actionable step you will take to unlock your leadership potential.

Chapter 7
Listen

> "I suggest that we may learn from spaces of silence as well as spaces of speech, that in the patient act of listening to another tongue we may subvert that culture of capitalist frenzy and consumption that demands all desire must be satisfied immediately…"
> — bell hooks

We must listen to one another to understand each other's choices, rather than challenge our differences in opinion. This is an idea I learned from staff members at poco, just after we re-opened to the public in 2022. At the time, I was chatting with one of the staff members about my relationship with my son, Jason, who was managing poco at the time. She listened intently, then hesitated before sharing something impactful. She told me that anytime she spoke to Jason, he would turn the conversation into an argument and challenge her expertise. She said communicating with him was draining and she would rather problem-solve on her own than face continuous confrontation with him. His communication left her feeling gaslit and ignored in the workplace. When I heard this, I immediately thought of my own behaviors, past and present, and how they show up in my children. And I considered what I know about gaslighting.

Gaslighting is the act of taking information you hear and manipulating it to confuse someone, make them question their reality, and/or challenge their ability to reason. My son was exhibiting the same bad habit I'd been working on for much of my adult life: questioning and challenging people who bring new (and sometimes unexpected) information to the table. My daughter, Jessica, holds me accountable by recognizing and helping me work through this issue when it sneaks back into my actions. Each time, I have to let her know I hear her by verbally acknowledging that I understand her message. Then I try to listen as deeply as possible while resisting my knee-jerk reactions. This deep listening is extremely hard work for most people, including myself. Sometimes, I have an urge to block my daughter out. Embarrassingly, mentally blocking people out is another old behavior I've worked hard to temper over the course of my life.

> The work of staying present, accepting who and what is in front of us, and deep listening, are all lifelong endeavors. They are not things to attempt once, check-off on our self-development list, and then move on from. Instead, we should practice them in our daily lives as much as possible.

Once I recognized how likely it was that I had subconsciously passed those negative behaviors — blocking people out and using questioning as a line of defense — to Jason, I could move past my initial reaction of being startled by new information. Now I could focus on the impact of those behaviors. In her book, *Unearthing Our Roots: Restorative Practices for Cultivating Spaces of Belonging,* Krista Pérez talks about the burden gaslighting places on those affected by it. Pérez also addresses the individual and community effects of gaslighting, especially between communities of color and systems of oppression.

"We carry an invisible burden due to these [gaslighting] experiences. We must choose to transform that burden (perhaps manifested in our anger and frustration regarding a lack of recognition and/or being bypassed) into abundance by honoring, acknowledging, and affirming ourselves in our present state. We are works in progress. We must find balance..."[12] Pérez also makes clear that we have an individual responsibility to recognize and transform the trauma we've caused through behaviors like gaslighting. In my work as a diversity, equity, inclusion, and accessibility (DEIA) executive, I have found this to be true.

> Refusing to listen to and acknowledge others can lead to gaslighting. Gaslighting erodes trust and relationships. We have an individual responsibility to recognize and address the trauma created by gaslighting.

It's important to note, as well, that language is power. With language, we have the power to restore integrity by acknowledging our unintentional impact on someone and realigning our words to match our actions. Furthermore, sometimes the best use of our language is to

---

12   Peréz, K. (2022). *Unearthing Our Roots: Restorative Practices for Cultivating Spaces of Belonging.* Blue Cactus Press.

recognize when to use it and when to remain quiet. Instead of using language to immediately question people and their realities, I've found it is better to withhold an initial reaction to new or shocking information, then attempt to hold space for the information coming toward us (even if we want to avoid it). In this way, we can more fully receive the information being relayed to us and engage in deeper listening.

I like to imagine listening as an apple: the parts of listening I don't want to engage with — negativity, criticism, or conflict — are the core. The parts I do want to engage with – compliments, storytelling, information gathering — are the flesh. Typically, when we eat an apple, we start from the outside and work our way inside, toward the core. Then, many of us throw the core away rather than consume it. But, if we turn the apple onto its side (stem facing to the right of the cutting board) and cut through the middle of the fruit, instead, we can consume the core along with the fruit with less discomfort. We'll end up with multiple rings of fruit, each with its own small pieces of pith and seed. I like to think of apple seeds as the lessons we learn, or what we discover, over the course of our lives.

Sure, this is a different method than we normally use for slicing and eating an apple, but nothing has changed about the apple, except our perspective. But now, with significantly less apple core in each slice, we can stand to eat the whole apple, core included, with less discomfort. Listening is like this. We can consume things (like new and unsavory information) that we typically avoid in conversation just as we would avoid consuming the core of an apple. By changing our behavior and shifting our perspective, we can more fully absorb a message we may desperately need to hear.

Last year, I was having dinner with my niece, Mia, and I was presented with an opportunity to put this framework into action. Mia and I are very close. At the time, we were on vacation together in Las Vegas. We were having dinner one evening and she and I got into a discussion about whether or not to tell folks we see in passing that they are beautiful for no other reason than to acknowledge their beauty. She didn't understand why I would tell someone that, and more specifically, why I would tell that to the couple sitting at the table in front of us, an older Black man and woman.

At first, I didn't want to hear Mia's perspective, which was that it was completely inappropriate for me to comment on people's appearance without a strong reason for doing so. My immediate reaction was to challenge her viewpoint and explain why I felt it necessary to compliment the older couple. But right then, an image of my daughter popped into my head, one of her face as she sees me struggling to withhold my initial reaction and knows I'm about to question everything, and I mean everything, coming out of someone's mouth. With that image fresh in my mind, I stopped myself from reacting and I closed my mouth. I tried to listen harder to my niece. I was ready to pop-off at any moment, but once my nerves settled, I realized something more important: Mia felt comfortable enough with me to speak up when she felt my actions weren't appropriate. I took a few breaths. I tried to soften my face and show her I was capable of listening, really listening, to her in the heat of a moment.

After hearing her out, in an attempt to ensure she felt listened to, I repeated what she had said. She was so surprised by my awareness that she acknowledged the moment between us. We were communicating well, across generations, in public, during a disagreement! To my surprise, Mia then used our open line of communication to share concerns about how I was living my life. I was taken aback. Mia told me that the amount of time I spend working is unhealthy and that my job keeps me small, despite the greatness she and other people in our life see within me. She told me that she knows I like to use personal insight from experience to inform my vision for organizations I work with, in my personal development, and in my intimate relationships. I love to dream and envision new ways of being and doing on this planet, and she has known that since she was a teenager. But from Mia's perspective, there was no place for that visionary work at my current job. She shared that she believes my job places a heavy and unnecessary burden on me. She told me I should quit my job and unburden myself!

Once I got past my shock at the turn in the conversation, I heard her. And I tried to show her that I heard her. I agreed that I needed to make a professional shift that would allow me to expand in all areas of my life, not just my work. By focusing on listening, I had the rare opportunity to be guided, mentored, and poured into by my wise and emboldened niece. If I had not listened to her initially and instead had just allowed my knee-jerk reactions to guide me through our interaction, I never would have shared this eye-opening experience with Mia or given her the opportunity to step into a leadership position in that conversation. By remaining open and acting as my best self, I was able to receive her as a more self-actualized version of herself.

Shortly after Mia and I returned from Las Vegas, I realized the only reason I hadn't quit my job yet was that I wanted to make a positive impact on our workplace culture and I had a lot of work to do if I wanted to make that happen. I was hell-bent on building a more inclusive culture, kicking doors down for people from historically marginalized groups, and altering how people relate to each other in this professional setting. I wanted to deepen the working relationships at our organization as deeply as I wanted to alter the relationships in my wider geographic and social communities. If I could make that happen, I could stomach sticking around for a while longer at my current organization.

A few days later, as clearly as I could, I shared my aspirations and my perspective on my particular role at the organization with my boss at the time. I also told my boss about my misgivings. She told me to take my time in determining whether I wanted to work toward my goal there. She asked me to give her, and my goal of changing the workplace culture, a minimum of eighteen months. Within that time, she said, she would remain loyal to me and my plans. She committed to working with me so long as I committed to her timeframe.

This was the first time in my entire career that a boss had sat me down to tell me they had my back. Not only is this boss a powerful woman, but she is also a Black woman. And she's the first Black woman I have ever worked for. She had never seemed a more powerful and charismatic leader than she did at that exact moment. When she told me she had my back, I believed her. And since then, our respective work has improved in the presence of our mutual commitment.

In our conversation, she practiced listening as I explained what I was trying to accomplish: affecting positive cultural change in the workplace. Did I still feel overworked and unable to "turn off" my work brain once I left the office? Yes. Did I still take on more stress and responsibility than other C-Suite managers at my organization? Yes. But since that conversation, I have had an easier time carrying my workload because I felt supported and cared for by my boss.

A few months down the line, I had another opportunity to check in with Mia about our conversation over dinner in Vegas. I told her about everything that happened at work. We both agreed that even though my work was placing a heavy burden on me, it was also deeply fulfilling and I felt particularly supported these days. And I didn't want to let that go just yet. Still, Mia had concerns about my sudden optimism. She had listened to countless gripe sessions over pizza and was fully aware of my work history at this organization. It was peppered with microaggressions, backstabbing, and painful situations that weighed me down over time. Mia wanted to save me from further pain and discomfort. Rightly so, as she understands how prone I am to giving too much of myself (not setting boundaries) in attempts to mentor and care for others. Mia also expressed that ultimately, she felt I was "buying into the corporate rat race."

As I listened to Mia's thoughts and took into account where her (very justified) fears for me originated, I came to understand that at the heart of the matter, Mia and my boss were sending the same message. Both saw the burden my work placed on me and were asking me to reconsider, but from different ends of the spectrum. My boss was asking me to bear a burden for a specific amount of time, with support, and see my work through. Mia saw the burden I was carrying and was asking me to lay it down, to walk away from an unnecessary hardship.

◇◇◇

Since then, I have continued to ask myself what this work means to me, and what it means to let go of my corporate career when it is so deeply connected to my values and desire to affect institutional change. I keep coming back to the same conclusion: After I fulfill my time commitment to my boss, I will shift my energy to cultivating an environment of inclusivity, which I so deeply desire in corporate America, in my entrepreneurial endeavors. I want to create culturally inclusive spaces that elevate people and their life's work. I believe fostering inclusivity is my calling. And I am thirsty to learn how to develop accessible spaces in light of ethnic, economic, and differently-bodied considerations. I believe deep listening is a key behavior that will allow me to do this work.

Luckily for me, building listening skills is facilitated by my natural curiosity toward people. Listening well is a necessary skill for me to carry out my purpose in life. I am fascinated by individuals and their stories. My fascination kicks into full gear when I get opportunities to learn about new people in my life who are from different cultural, generational, or experiential backgrounds. Truly listening makes space for them to bring their full selves into a conversation. By leaning into conversation, I can recognize our similarities and build empathy between us. I can see that we are all deserving of equal time and consideration.

> By paying attention to how we are all connected, rather than how we are not, we can remain open to more information and build our listening skills. Here, we grow *with* each other, not away from each other.

We are extensions of each other. Each of us is an interconnected participant in the natural world. Leaning into this perspective helps us understand how we can authentically contribute to the greater network of people on Earth. This vision of inclusivity drives me forward. I am doing my best to embrace the journey. As I take steps forward in my life, I must deal with my demons one at a time. I must not let those demons — in this case, poor listening, discounting relevant information, doubting expertise, being confrontational, and gaslighting — keep me or anyone else small. I must remain as open and receptive as possible while engaging with others. This is how we cultivate listening skills and embrace diversity of thought.

> As we listen to the thoughts in our heads, we gain clarity about ourselves, the people around us, and the situation at hand. We can look at a situation from different perspectives, which (probably) more accurately reflect the full scope of the situation at hand.

key takeaways

- 🔓 The work of staying present, accepting who and what is in front of us, and deep listening, are all lifelong endeavors. They are not things to attempt once, check-off on our self-development list, and then move on from. Instead, we should practice them in our daily lives.

- 🔓 Refusing to listen to and acknowledge others can lead to gaslighting. Gaslighting erodes trust and relationships. We have an individual responsibility to recognize and address the trauma created by gaslighting.

- 🔓 By paying attention to how we are all connected, rather than how we are not, we can remain open to more information and build our listening skills. Here, we grow *with* each other, not *away* from each other.

- 🔓 As we listen to the thoughts in our heads, we gain clarity about ourselves, the people around us, and the situation at hand. We can look at a situation from different perspectives, which (probably) more accurately reflect the full scope of the situation at hand.

transformative learning space

Consider what you read in this chapter and the key takeaways listed above. Write down a few ideas about how you can you apply these learning points to your own leadership practice. Include at least one actionable step you will take to unlock your leadership potential.

Chapter 8
Gain & Provide Clarity

> "If you don't have clarity of ideas, you're just communicating sheer sound."
>
> — Yo-Yo Ma

Clarity helps us manifest the things we truly desire in life. If we do not gain clarity on what those things are, and if we do not communicate our desire for them, we trap energy within ourselves. Or we blindly follow our ambition at the cost of other important aspects of our lives, like our relationships with family. When we do gain clarity about our truths and express them through clear and open communication, we let our energy expand. We give ourselves space to breathe and permission to step into our fullest power.

> Clarity leads to self-truth and authenticity, both of which are necessary for the success of relationship building.

Authenticity allows us to embrace others enough to build partnerships and community with them. Being authentic looks like letting people see who we are, deep down at our core, and showing people our most vulnerable selves despite knowing we may get hurt in the process. Allowing ourselves to demonstrate vulnerability like this is one of the hardest things we can practice in our lifetime, as it pushes us to embrace uncertainty and situations that tend to lead us (uncomfortably) toward learning and growth. Yet all of this is essential to building strong relationships.

When we withhold vulnerability, we hide significant and essential parts of our psyche that have probably done us a lot of good in our lives. Those parts tend to include our hopes, fears, doubts, and excitements. If we cannot trust the people around us enough to lay bare those parts of ourselves to them, we will be alone on our journey through life (I'm talking about our *real* journey here, not the sugarcoated version we display on social media or in public spheres).

We must also make efforts to understand who our loved ones are and why they do things the way they do. But just as before, we must first gain clarity about those same aspects of ourselves. Otherwise, our lack of clarity or self-awareness will get in the way of seeing others for who they are.

> When we lack clarity, we create space for doubt and fear to creep into the "unknown" corners of our minds and negatively shape the stories we tell ourselves.

Inevitably, fear and doubt lead us to push people away. It undermines our relationships. But if we acknowledge the truths of the people we love alongside our own truths, we honor them. And most of us desire to honor and be in community with others. We crave giving and receiving the support we know is necessary for our well-being. Engaging in this give-and-take of support includes building and dreaming with others, voicing expectations, and being truthful about our desires. It also means reaching out to our networks to establish meaningful connections. As Amber Cabral reminded me during our podcast recording, "Leveraging your network during critical professional moments is key." To do so, we must first have a clear mind, clear motivations, and a thorough understanding of the desires and motivations of those we care about. We gain that clarity through self-reflection.

Self-reflection can look like asking ourselves questions about the what's, why's, and how's behind our actions. If we can't answer those questions, we probably don't have true clarity about a situation. But once we reflect enough to answer those questions and feel, in our gut, that we know how to proceed, we can move forward with a purpose. Once we set our purpose, we can align ourselves and others to it, then pool resources toward that shared purpose. Everyone will feel connected to the shared goal. This is important, as connection fosters inspiration, and inspiration is necessary for achieving our goals.

When we move forward without clarity, people are likely to make assumptions about our alignment and intent. We can't blame them for doing so if we fail to give them the information they want. Worse yet, if we then fall short of their expectations, they will lose faith in us. If you find yourself in a situation where someone is confused about your intent; if you have fallen short of someone's expectations; and/or if you have not been able to speak your truth to someone; then pause and reflect on the situation at hand. Consider how you might be out of alignment with your values or commitments.

> If you find yourself out of alignment with your values and/or commitments, reflect, then make changes to realign with your values. In most cases, realigning with your values will not be a quick process. Do not push forward too quickly or too hard. Let the process take as long as it needs to.

The Trust Model, which I introduced in the last chapter, is a helpful tool for visualizing the leadership skills and values necessary for gaining the information you need to realign with your values and move back into a trusting dynamic with those around you. As we can see from the Trust Model, seeking clarity like this is a part of active listening, which is necessary to move toward trust.

key takeaways

- Clarity leads to self-truth and authenticity, both of which are necessary to the success of relationship building.

- When we lack clarity, we create space for doubt and fear to creep into the "unknown" corners of our minds and negatively shape the stories we tell ourselves.

- If you find yourself out of alignment with your values and/or commitments, reflect, then make changes to realign with your values. In most cases, realigning with your values will not be a quick process. Do not push forward too quickly or too hard. Let the process take as long as it needs to.

transformative learning space

Consider what you read in this chapter and the key takeaways listed above. Write down a few ideas about how you can you apply these learning points to your own leadership practice. Include at least one actionable step you will take to unlock your leadership potential.

case study

Gaining Clarity & Building a Shared Vision at poco
by Jesse Rhodes Jr.

A few months after opening poco, I finally had the time and headspace to focus on event programming. I wanted to use events as a vehicle for my larger vision of poco and what it could mean to the communities it served. I knew that if I wanted to see my vision brought to life, I would have to plant the seeds for it before it was possible for it to come to fruition. In particular, I wanted poco to become an accessible and welcoming event venue for people in our neighborhood and the wider geographic community. I hoped to create a space where people could convene and cultivate cross-cultural relationships and communication strategies; where parents and teachers could find support; and where people could nourish their bodies and minds.

As you know from my earlier stories about poco, I failed to convey this vision to staff when we opened the restaurant. A few months later, once we'd all settled into our roles, I tried again. I set up a meeting with the staff. This time, I was sure I could establish a shared vision of poco and the impact I wanted to have on our community. On the day of the meeting, I rehearsed my pitch to the staff. I arrived early. I made copies of my plan in anticipation of a vibrant discussion. When the meeting started, I shared a list of upcoming, tentative events we'd host at poco over the next four months. The list was long, though carefully curated.

The information and events list did not land well with staff. As they looked over the list, I delivered my pitch about crafting a hearty events calendar and connecting with the community. The more I talked, the quieter the room became.

Pretty soon, the room was so quiet I could hear people shifting in their chairs and folding up the events calendar I'd so carefully printed out. After some prodding, a few staff members finally spoke up. They were not used to such a packed event schedule. The room then fell back into an uneasy silence. I could tell there was something else at play, some unspoken narrative I had yet to tease out of them, but I could not get past the wall that had quietly appeared between myself and the staff. I tried pushing forward, but for the rest of our time together, staff participation was reduced to almost zero. There was palpable resistance to my plan, but no one would speak up to explain why.

Still, I pushed on. I walked the staff through my entire strategy again, in the hopes that they had missed some critical information. Ultimately, I was unable to connect with staff in any meaningful way during that meeting. I didn't understand why they were so resistant to and tight-lipped about my plan. I thought it was an uncomplicated strategy, but if that was the case, why were the vibes so off during the meeting? Why did it seem like no one else was on board with my idea? I thought it wise to pause before putting my plan into action. There was no harm in waiting, and I could always return to the event conversation at a later date.

A few weeks went by before I tried another approach to events programming with the staff. This time, I met with senior staff members and my management team in a one-on-one environment. It was in these meetings that I finally learned why I wasn't able to get buy-in from the staff: They saw the event schedule and assumed that more events meant more work for them. They didn't understand why we were pushing so hard for events as a revenue stream. Or why we needed to push so hard so fast. They couldn't see that carrying out events was how I wanted to connect with our wider community. Or that much of the work of planning and executing event-specific needs would fall to managers and higher-level staff. I had failed to bring adequate clarity to my vision at our initial meeting about events. Staff told me that when we discussed event programming, I had also used language that they either didn't understand or did not resonate with them. They felt that my language, and I, by extension, was too corporate. The language I was using and the persona I moved through the world with felt completely foreign to them. All they could see (and react to) was a wildly busy event calendar that I had dropped in their lap.

I went home that night and thought about all the ways I had not only failed to communicate my message but placed my staff outside of the very community I was trying to build and connect with. I gave myself time to feel my emotions fully. I let myself experience some self-pity, then I emotionally regrouped. I brainstormed how I could return to the conversation and attempt to make my intentions clear to the staff. I could use language that wasn't coded with corporate jargon. I could simplify my vision. I could start planning events slowly, then gradually increase the events on our schedule as staff acclimated to the pacing. More than anything else, I wanted to make sure staff understood that more events didn't necessarily mean more work; it meant more *connection* during existing work hours. It meant more *publicity* with the media. And it meant more *opportunities* to create an atmosphere and culture of inclusivity and comfort.

Once I solidified my new approach, I scheduled another meeting with my staff. This time, I was sure I would get through to them. When the time for our meeting came, I presented my information as clearly as I could, using language I'd heard them use before. Then, I invited them to share their visions of success with me. I asked them what they wanted to create in the short term, what they wanted to build over time, and how they might relay that through service, food, and drink. What did poco, as a physical place and philosophical idea, mean to them? And how could we accomplish their goals and mine at the same time? Did they believe that was even possible? And what did they need from me to bring this new vision — which we created together — to fruition? As embarrassing as it sounds, I probably engaged in more listening during that meeting than I had in the entire month preceding it. But by listening intently, asking for more information, and actively listening to what staff had to say, I was able to make incredible headway toward my goal: getting staff buy-in for a heavier event schedule. More importantly, the staff helped me define the values and mission of poco, as well as formulate the meaning behind "poco:" Purposeful. Organic. Captivating. Optimistic. That day, I was reminded of the power of clarity and the necessity of continuously honing one's listening skills. In the end, we moved forward with the plan we created together, and a shared vision that was much bigger than any of our individual ideas.

Chapter 9
Fulfill Commitments

"The road to success is through commitment."
— Will Smith

When we make commitments, people watch to see if we follow through on them. If we want to change or move on from something, we either need to fulfill the original contract or adjust the terms before taking action. If we don't complete (or at the very least address) the things we've committed to but have yet to fulfill, they will hold us back from moving forward on our life's journey. We will stop growing and will become stagnant. This is what happens when we are unable to bridge our words with our actions. We move no closer to self-actualization. Our unfulfilled commitments will restrict our ability to be present with what is right in front of us. They will keep our minds focused on what is behind us and in our past.

It's tempting to think we can put off taking action to re-focus on fulfilling our commitments. We might hide our procrastination in circular or unending self-reflection. We may not realize our overzealous reading about and researching challenges can shift us to a state of avoidance. The bottom line is, though, if we perpetually table our challenges to search for solutions, we are choosing inaction. To find a resolution, to fulfill our commitments, we must choose action. Moving toward resolution must be a priority. We must take charge of our life's journey, fill in our map of life as we want to live it, select our routes, and make hard decisions. Otherwise, we become passive bystanders in our own lives and jeopardize our integrity in the eyes of people who care for us.

> We can maintain our integrity, especially when we are unable to take immediate action toward our goals, by being people of our word and fulfilling our commitments.

There will be times in our lives when all we have is our words and the meaning they impart to ourselves and others. This is why it is important to be careful with our words. Thankfully, language is powerful, and we can use it to weave our desired futures into existence. The power of language can move us from inaction to action. It can free us from living out storylines that do not benefit us, and even help us craft new storylines for our lives.

> If we want to change our lives, we begin by changing the words we use in our storylines.

◇◇◇

Now, let's dive into what happens when we don't move toward fulfilling our commitments, whatever the reason. When this happens, the cost can be significant. Financially, our inaction might result in accrued interest on unpaid bills, late fees, bad credit, or loss of property. In relationships, it may result in neglect of the needs of our loved ones or refusal to acknowledge the pain we've caused. In personal development, it may manifest as a negative self-image and narratives we repeat to ourselves, such as not believing we will be successful, or imposter syndrome, or self-sabotaging our endeavors because staying small is safer than taking risks.

Let me offer myself as an example. As an accountant, I love to make spreadsheets and profit and loss statements for both my personal and business finances. Last autumn, I realized I hadn't created a balance sheet or profit and loss statement for myself in over three months! I usually love this kind of work, so when I realized I had been neglecting my finances for months, hell, even a season, I knew something was up. I had built conflict for myself and cultivated a lack of clarity around my finances. Not to mention, this was at a pivotal time in my life. I was in the middle of renovating poco and my finances needed to be rock solid. I needed financial clarity. I knew having it would give me the confidence necessary to make in-the-moment decisions about investing my money at poco. But because my finances were a mess, I couldn't even develop a basic financial strategy, let alone act on it. My lack of commitment to organizing my finances was beginning to hold me back in other areas of my life. As far as I could tell, I was broke. My cashflow had slowed to a mere trickle and I couldn't travel, take my children to dinner, or treat myself to a massage or pedicure. I had to ask myself some hard questions.

Am I really broke or do I have more money coming my way?
What am I avoiding by not gathering this information proactively?
What is my relationship with money and control right now?

Why am I letting a perceived lack of money hold me back, especially at a time when I need to commit to taking a huge leap forward with my new business?

In answering these questions for myself, I discovered I was carrying baggage from past business ventures alongside the weight and responsibility of my new business. I thought I'd moved on from those business challenges, yet here I was, in a similar predicament to one I'd faced before: I was going broke at a critical point in my entrepreneurial endeavor. When I finally sat down and went over my finances, I discovered I wasn't actually broke. I was just forcing myself to live in financial scarcity because it allowed me to *believe* I was broke. This belief was reinforced by my lack of knowledge about my cash flow and the current standing of my resources. Every time I refused to review my finances or look critically at my cash flow, I could hold onto the storyline that I was broke and couldn't afford to move forward with my plans. Holding onto this storyline was a convenient way to allow my fear and avoidance to keep me stagnant.

I reflected on one of my past business ventures in which I'd experienced something similar. When I was younger, for example, I established a business with my wife at the time. When we opened the business, we were happily married. But shortly after we reached our version of success, our marriage became fraught with stress and strife. Even though we'd found early success in our business, my wife felt neglected in her role there, and she felt alone. The reality of her isolation didn't align with her expectation of how we'd agreed to carry out our daily work at the organization. From her perspective, I was not following through with the commitment I'd made to her: to work together in our new venture. Unfortunately, I was still working a traditional nine-to-five job in a corporate setting when we opened our business. That meant most of my involvement with our business happened from a distance. Meanwhile, my wife spent her time working directly in the business, managing day-to-day operations. Because of this, we weren't as connected in carrying out our work as we thought we would be. And, we were not adept at checking-in with each other to make sure we were moving in the same direction.

Unsurprisingly, our personal and professional challenges began to compound. Then, the economy went into recession and we began losing contracts we depended on to pay staff at our business. Working together amidst all this emotional and financial strife became too much for my wife and me to bear. We could both see the writing on the wall: Our business would probably close if we could not realign and fulfill our commitments to one another.

As the situation unfolded, I took on the emotional weight of every marriage, parenting, and business "failure" I could think of. I included the business we shared, which was meant to serve as the vehicle for my early retirement, in my list of failures. Truth be told, I had a lot more than money riding on the success of our venture. Not only was it meant to provide my retirement income, but it was supposed to provide an opportunity for me to move away from corporate America and toward more time with my family. I wanted to be more present in my children's lives, and managing the business would allow me to do that. I had planned to keep the business open until my children (who were still young at the time of our divorce) grew into adults. I dreamed of being right beside them as they navigated college and adulthood. I had it all planned out.

Unfortunately, as we all know, our best-laid plans can and often do go up in flames. Unsurprisingly, the working relationship between my wife and I began to deteriorate. It became abundantly clear to everyone in our organization that we could not co-manage the business while also dealing with strife in our marriage. So, we decided to close the business. I reached out to my father. He had helped me overcome adversity in the past, and I'd hoped he could help me again. My father had taught me that in our darkest moments, our community will surely pull us through *if we let it*. During my divorce, my father stepped up and into that community position. He offered me help when I needed it most, and when I was most likely to isolate myself because of shame of my perceived failures. My father talked to me about fortitude, or, in his words, the strength of mind that enables a person to encounter danger or to bear pain with coolness and courage. He gifted me one of his service badges, too, as a symbol of the fortitude I needed to embody to properly address, troubleshoot, and move through this tribulation.

Fast forward to last autumn, the eve of poco's opening, when I confronted my refusal to deal with my finances. I found that if I wanted to play down the storyline of being broke and stagnant, my personal development work was to "clean up my parking lot," or my mental space. "Cleaning up my parking lot," as Sam Rosario and Bilal Babwani call it in Rosario's book, *The Super Productive Leader: Time Management Strategies for the Digital Age*[13], is akin to tidying your headspace, then building a mental database of tasks you need to accomplish your goals. If you have the capacity, you can deepen the exercise by categorizing the tasks according to your personal needs.

In my case, I needed to clean up my parking lot so I could move past a storyline that kept me small and stuck. I needed to confront how my current actions (ignoring my finances) were similar to those I'd made when my wife and I were navigating the eminent closure of our business. With reflection, I saw that refusing to handle my finances kept me from gaining the mental clarity I needed to push poco toward success. And I recognized that I was still emotionally wallowing in self-flagellation over my past "failures." If I wanted to move forward with poco, I had to release myself from the guilt, the pain, and the blame I'd heaped onto my shoulders for closing down the business I'd started with my wife. I needed to commit to self-healing and take action toward that reality. I could not stay committed to the ghosts of my past while also committing to the vision of my future: poco.

---

[13] Rosario, S. (2023). *The Super Productive Leader: Time Management Strategies for the Digital Age.*

> We cannot cling to the visions of our past while also committing to the visions of our future.

I often return to the "parking lot" metaphor because it makes me and whoever I'm talking to smile. We all have mental "parking lots" that relate to some aspect of our lives. The things in our parking lots are not usually new. They tend to be past trauma, pain, or unresolved emotions we've collected from lived experiences. We might linger in one parking lot all day, thinking about this or that unresolved issue or emotion while ignoring others. But we can't let trauma, pain, fear, self-doubt, resentment, or any other emotions we've got locked away keep us from committing to and acting on our truest desires. We must unpack our experiences, then release what we're holding onto so we can make space for new things. Then we can move forward with clarity and intention. By fulfilling our commitments, we move toward self-actualization.

key takeaways

- 🔓 We can maintain our integrity, especially when we are unable to take immediate action toward our goals, by being people of our word and fulfilling our commitments.

- 🔓 If we want to change our lives, we begin by changing the words we use in our storylines.

- 🔓 We cannot cling to the visions of our past while also committing to the visions of our future.

transformative learning space

Consider what you read in this chapter and the key takeaways listed above. Write down a few ideas about how you can you apply these learning points to your own leadership practice. Include at least one actionable step you will take to unlock your leadership potential.

case study

Living Life Inspired by Purpose
by Kaplan Mobray

Kaplan Mobray is an award-winning author, speaker, and career consultant. He is the author of The 10Ks of Personal Branding.

One of the most powerful aspects of your purpose is the mindset that inspires it to take shape in your life. There will come a moment in your life that will grip you and challenge you to do something out of your comfort zone. That moment and season of your life will inspire you to take on a new opportunity, devote your time and energy to creating a powerful result to help someone in need, or create a once unimaginable possibility. That moment will reveal to you why you were placed on this earth and why your life and all that you do matter. This moment is called purpose. And it happens "on purpose."

I can reflect on my journey of embracing purpose with crystal clarity. For me, it happened after giving a presentation to a group of students while guest lecturing at a university. What was supposed to be a one-time presentation offering career advice and mentoring to students on how to build their personal brand turned into a life-changing moment. During my presentation, I talked about the power of being intentional and consistent. I challenged the students in the audience with the question: What do you want to be known for? I stated that if you don't have a personal brand, you may not be memorable to others who are in a position to grant you opportunities. I further stated that if you are not memorable, others may discount your value, which could limit your potential to advance in your career. I could see their minds turning and thinking and trying to solve the riddle of how well they knew themselves and if they knew their brand.

Following the presentation, a student waited for everyone to clear out before approaching me and sharing these words:

"You changed my life."

I'll never forget the feeling of earnestness the student exuded while sharing how he was going to use the tools I offered to overhaul his approach to living life and growing his career. Hearing those words activated a new mission for me. I thought to myself,

If I can change one person's life, then maybe I have a responsibility and opportunity to help more people. To change more lives, to make a bigger difference in the world.

This revelation inspired me to leave my corporate job, (a job I loved) and set out on a journey to start speaking to more audiences. I wanted to motivate people and teach them how to grow their career and build their personal brand. It was this same inspiration that encouraged me to later write my award-winning book, *The 10Ks of Personal Branding*. With that book, I took my very first presentation and made it a guide to help others change their life and career circumstances.

Now, I've spent over a decade speaking to audiences all over the world, across six continents. Each time, I return to the power of purpose. The day I shared my first "10Ks of Personal Branding" presentation to a group of students was a day of activation. Hearing those words, "You changed my life," was a moment that activated my purpose. I left that room changed. Changed by the words I shared and the words that were shared with me.

But for me to activate my purpose I had to listen to the bigger message behind the feedback on the presentation. I had to accept that there was now more to do. And this effort was just the beginning of a larger journey. It was bigger than me. I had to embrace a mindset of gratitude for the assignment I was given to help change more people's lives for the better. And I had to commit to the effort, sacrifice, time, and courage that would be required of me to walk in the power and activation of my purpose.

I am often asked the question, How did you discover your purpose? And what lessons can others learn from your journey? I respond by saying I listened, I accepted, I am grateful, and I made a commitment.

Listen. Accept. Be grateful. Be committed.

If you are on the journey to find your purpose, or if you have found it but are looking for a way to activate it beyond what you are doing today, here are the words of encouragement I offer to you:

Purpose happens "on purpose"

Your purpose will find you or you will find it. You might be able to control or predict the timing and the circumstances. However, when you find it, you will know, and you will be presented with the choice to listen, accept, be grateful, and make a commitment.

Recognize the signature moments in your life that give you an opportunity to create a greater impact on someone's life, to endure a challenge that gives you new learnings, which will thereby allow you to face life with new courage and renewed conviction. Recognize the moments that take your breath away. Those moments created a way for you to understand your own significance. Notice when you just cannot let go of the desire to change something for the better and you will not stop until you know that it has changed. They say things happen for a reason. Let your purpose give you purpose. Because purpose happens "on purpose."

Listen to your "unconscious voice"

Often, your purpose lives within you well before you have the courage to listen to it. It's a voice inside you that provokes you with tough questions about your life and how you are spending your time. It's that inner voice challenging you to be a better version of yourself in what you do and how you do it. For example, you may be working in a job or career field that does not fulfill you. It may be causing you pain and mental anguish. And for that reason, you have always wanted to do something that gives more meaning to your life and those around you. That unconscious voice is telling you that there is a greater purpose for your life. However, there are plenty of reasons you might block your inner voice, or resist listening to it. At some point, though, you will encounter a trigger moment. It could be health-related, a personal situation, a career transition, or a life crossroad. Suddenly, you will be faced with an opportunity to listen to that unconscious voice within you as it once again asks the question, "What are you doing with your life?"

This is a common scenario for many of the individuals and leaders I coach and counsel. The one common denominator when speaking with these individuals is that when they arrived at understanding their purpose, many have said they knew it all along. They just needed the push, the disruption, the unexpected twist of life to give them the reflection to face and listen to that powerful unconscious voice within. What is your inner voice telling you about your purpose? Are you listening?

Accept the gift of gratitude

One of the greatest gifts you can receive is your ability to accept life's gift of gratitude. Gratitude for your life and your unique experiences is a gift that allows you to offer a perspective that can help someone else. You have greater access to your purpose when you are grounded in gratitude. This means taking time to be intentional about acknowledging what you are grateful for. The big things, the small things, the experiences in your past, the hopefulness of your future... the risks that you took that did not work out, and the courage you embraced to achieve a major milestone. Be grateful for it all.

When you pronounce your gratitude for life, you also acknowledge that your life has meaning. Your life gave you something to be thankful for, and this is a powerful reminder of the purpose of your journey. So, if you are looking to find or refine your purpose in life, start by being vocal about the things that you are grateful for. It will give you inspired energy. And you will become an inspiration for someone in the future. Accept the gift so you can become the gift.

Be committed to the journey, not just the awakening

Walking a path of purpose is a commitment. It's easy to find your purpose, acknowledge it, be grateful for it, and then get stuck because of the heaping work, time, sacrifice, effort, and selflessness it takes to keep the journey of your purpose alive. But that's exactly what purpose demands. Walking in your purpose means making a binding agreement with yourself to maintain the energy and inspiration that sustains meaning and a sense of fulfillment in your life. Commitment to your purpose requires sustained action doing the things that give your life meaning. That might include making a difference, finding ways to create a profound impact on someone, or furthering a cause that is bigger than yourself. A commitment to purpose also requires an energy source. What do you do to refuel passion for your purpose? If you don't ask yourself this question, or create an answer for it in your life, it can be easy to burn out or to let your purpose fade.

So if you accept the challenge, responsibility, and honor of walking a path of purpose, bring with you the work ethic and source of joy that comes with doing what you are supposed to be doing. Be committed to the journey, not just the awakening. The journey to finding or refining your purpose is honorable. Make sure to embrace it not only for what your purpose does for you but for the monumental impact that you can have on the lives of others. In life, you get one lap, but you have to run the race, no matter what. In all you do as you walk the path of purpose, be inspired for the journey. Be the gift that keeps giving.

Live life by decision, not by default.

Part 3
Realizing Your Potential

Chapter 10
Inspire

> "Open heart, open mind... allows for endless possibilities."
> — MC Lyte

I understand how easy it is to lose ourselves as we set out to achieve our goals. We get so excited that we spring into action, allowing tunnel vision to keep us focused on resources that move us closer or further away from where we want to be, and almost nothing else. We begin to think we *own* things and that we are *owed* something in this life. But nothing is owed to us. We must work anew for our success each day. I define spiritual success as an alignment of values and actions on a day-to-day basis. As long as we maintain that alignment, we will naturally move closer to our goals each day. The first challenge is cultivating the fertile ground necessary for living a value-based life and not losing sight of gratitude along the way. This is the soil from which personal success grows and from which mentorship springs.

In corporate leadership settings, I hold an obligation, especially as a person of color, to remove the boardroom door for those who follow in my footsteps. "I hold an obligation" is another way of saying, "I am committed to remaining in alignment with my value of building equity in corporate leadership settings." I try not to allow myself to get too comfortable in a leadership position, as tempting as it may be, because I do not want to professionally plateau. When I feel that inertia setting in, I try to rekindle the fires of my ambition, which are built on a desire for collective growth. Sometimes that looks like mentoring others as they embark on a personal development journey or nurturing the technical expertise of direct reports. Bringing others up alongside us, in whatever position we might hold, can deliver a satisfaction deeper than any we've experienced before.

In communities of color, as well as in corporate settings, we must redefine "success" by creating new pathways that lead to positive outcomes. Just as importantly, we must consult elders and youth along the way. My brilliant daughter, Jessica, loves to remind me of this. She has taught me over the years that we must acknowledge the intellect and expertise of our youth and our elders, people who are usually pushed to the side and forgotten in mainstream American culture. Yet we desperately need the insight of these communities. With their knowledge, experience, and perspectives, we can learn how to better leverage resources toward inspiring others. We will only achieve success by working together after consulting with a diversity of people and perspectives.

We should also keep in mind that although our past experiences will inform the present, we must not let them pigeonhole us. We should strive to protect ourselves from stumbling over the same cracks we tripped on yesterday. We should leverage what we learned from those experiences to inform our current behavior. We, as individuals, get to define whether those past experiences were positive or negative, no one else. The stories we live in are written and repeated by ourselves. And we can use those stories, and what we've learned from our past experiences, as opportunities to revisit our goals, strategies, and behaviors with a critical eye. We can also use them to attempt to restore our integrity. If we remain open to the lessons our past taught us, we can coach others, as well, as we pull them up alongside us.

> True leadership is empowering others to achieve their goals while simultaneously working toward our own.

Alongside empowerment is inspiration. How do we inspire people to act once they have the resources and guidance necessary to move forward? This is an age-old question that countless corporate executives, community leaders, boards of directors, business owners, executive coaches, and philosophers ask themselves daily. It's a question most people face at least once in their lifetime. In my experience, the solution is different for each person. But I believe the root of all solutions lies buried in ourselves. To understand what inspires others, we first must understand what inspires us. The following are five principles that continue to inspire me in my journey as a thought leader in corporate and business cultures. I call them The Five Ps of Personal Development.

The Five Ps of Personal Development

Patience: Have patience and trust in the fact that whatever you need to succeed has been with you all along. If you're patient enough to sit with your thoughts, to acknowledge your fears, hopes, and motivations, you will uncover the key to your success.

Purpose: Gain clarity on what your purpose in life is. Knowing your purpose will attract others to follow you through the turmoil of personal and professional changes.

People: No one is alone on their journey. Embrace working with others and earnestly consider their input. Empower them to take action toward a shared vision of success. When it is your time for action, honor your word. Let your actions become the driving inspirational force for others.

Presence: Remain present for what comes up for you, emotionally and intellectually, at any given moment. Practice gratitude toward those emotions, ideas, and boundaries.

Persistence: Learn to be comfortable with receiving *no* as an answer. You will face an incredible number of *no*s and closed doors in your professional career. After receiving a *no*, pick yourself up, learn from it, and return to the drawing board. Endurance is key.

◇◇◇

It's time to circle back to an important topic: vulnerability.

> When we are vulnerable with others, they are more likely to empathize with us.

Empathy is a key ingredient to building strong relationships. It is also one of the cornerstones of inspiring others. Many people feel vulnerable when they share past moments of pain or elation. Although we tend to keep these memories hidden away, they are the golden nuggets of vulnerability and are the moments we are most likely to learn from. Therefore, we must allow others to see our pain, mistakes, frustrations, joys, and successes. When we do so, we allow others to see us as fallible. This knocks over the pedestal we, as leaders, are often placed on in corporate settings. Without the pedestal, we are just another person moving through the world and its infinite possibilities. We face the same challenges as those around us, only with a different perspective or story.

The more often we share our story or truth, the more we emphasize (internally and externally) that our truth matters in this world. Just as importantly, speaking our truths gives others space to do the same. By continuously being vulnerable with people in this way, we build trust and deepen our relationships. And when trust is the foundation of a relationship, we can use it to inspire others. Speaking our truth clarifies our story for others, shutting down the (often erroneous) narratives they've built about us. This clarification of our narrative, or story, allows us to set clear parameters with others and make collective decisions based on good faith, accurate information, and trust.

key takeaways

- True leadership is empowering others to achieve their goals while simultaneously working toward our own.

- The Five Ps of Personal Development are Patience, Purpose, People, Presence, and Persistence.

- When we are vulnerable with others, they are more likely to empathize with us, and consequently, to build a stronger relationship with us. This is the foundation of inspiring others.

transformative learning space

Consider what you read in this chapter and the key takeaways listed above. Write down a few ideas about how you can you apply these learning points to your own leadership practice. Include at least one actionable step you will take to unlock your leadership potential.

case study

You Can Have Whatever You Want
by Amber Cabral

Amber Cabral is an award-winning inclusion strategist, certified coach, TED speaker, and author of Allies and Advocates *and* Say More About That.

Looking back on my life, I can say I have always been entrepreneurial, but I just assumed that entrepreneurial spirit was part of my leadership style. You see, I have always been a tinkerer. I've always had ideas I wanted to bring to life. I was content doing so within organizations as long as I had the kind of boss who would make room for me to implement those ideas and be curious about ways to improve whatever I was working on. What I didn't expect was that I would one day start a company that would routinely gross one to three million dollars annually under my leadership. That wasn't on my bingo card. But let me go back to 2017 when all of this started.

It was January. I was working at Walmart at the time, and it was a great place to "do corporate." While I was there, I had the opportunity to build things, grow strong relationships, work under leaders — both strong and not — and launch new ideas. I built resources and programming for a global mentoring program; I led, grew, and diversified the corporate intern program; and I helped build and roll out a culture transformation project that centered equity and landed me in the role I thought I was going to remain in for a good long while: Diversity Strategist. But purpose is a certain derailer. And my purpose was getting ready to pull me in a whole different direction.

My sweet spot at Walmart turned unexpectedly sour in ways I couldn't have predicted. There I was, working at Walmart and living in Northwest Arkansas, (or as I called it, Nowhere, Arkansas) when my life unraveled. That unraveling only took about 45 days. I was at the strangest of odds with the leadership and no longer trusted my team. My romantic relationship ended terribly and over the phone. I left Walmart, and Arkansas (with a severance package, thank goodness). And then I was sexually assaulted.

2017 started out so ... YIKES. And truthfully, I kind of lost it for a moment. I decided to put all my stuff in storage. And because I didn't know where else to go, I moved into my godparent's house in Dallas, Texas, to figure my life out. I had a number of interviews lined up with companies that most people would leap for joy to work for, so I felt good about the prospect of being back on my feet in no time. Boy was I wrong.

By April of 2017, I realized I was still interviewing for jobs. As in, those interviews I had lined up in January?... None of them had landed yet. Throughout that process, I never got a rejection for a role I interviewed for – not a single one. But every job I interviewed for seemed to end up on hold or postponed or canceled. In two cases, the organization that wanted to hire me was also trying to source the person who would be my leader. But I just wasn't willing to accept a role without knowing who I would be reporting to. So, offers had been extended to me, but I was waiting to accept them contingent on having an opportunity to interview with my leader. It was a bizarre job search, but because the opportunities were with reputable companies, I was optimistic. Still, I was exhausted.

I had just found a therapist to help me process everything that happened in January, so it was a very odd place to be emotionally. A dear friend of mine, who was also still working for Walmart but was on an assignment in China, flew me to China to recover. Once I was on the other side of the world, I hopped around Asia for a few weeks, recovering emotionally and spiritually. When I returned to the U.S., I doubled down on the job hunt.

By the end of May, I was so frustrated with the process of looking for a job. The cycle was the same as before I'd left for China. I would land an initial job interview. Then, after the second interview, I would go tell my God-dad about the position. He'd listen patiently and then ask me,

"Is this a job that you want?"

For the longest time, my answer was always the same. "I mean, I really want to stop sleeping in y'all's theater room."

He'd always tell me, "No one is rushing you. Take a job that you want, not just any job."

I didn't really hear him clearly until after multiple weeks of this cycle. It wasn't until I was in the middle of an interview one day when the leader of the organization I was applying to asked if I had any questions, that I finally heard my God-dad.

"I do, actually. Can you share with me what professional development looks like for this role? How will you ensure that I continue to learn and grow so I can bring that knowledge into the company?"

"Great question! There is no outside development opportunity with this role, like attending conferences or programs. We bring talent in-house, and you would be exposed to those resources as your development."

Her answer set off a light switch in my mind. I immediately knew I didn't want to work there. So, I politely thanked the interviewer for her time and shared that I would like to remove myself from the candidate pool for the role because external development opportunities were important to me. The interviewer was too stunned to speak. She stumbled over a couple of sentences before finally thanking me for my time. We ended the interview.

I was emotional. I cried when I got home and then went downstairs to tell my God-dad what happened.

He listened, then said, "Good. It didn't sound like what you wanted."

"It wasn't. But I am not sure I know what I want as much as I know what I don't want."

"Well, people don't often get time like you have now to figure it out, so think about it. You can have whatever you want."

And boom. A mantra was born: You can have whatever you want. Sometimes I shorten the phrase to the acronym YCHWYW. Starting that day, I began asking myself what I wanted. Answering was hard. Like most folks, I lived my life mostly selecting from what was presented to me. I hadn't ever sat down and considered what I wanted. How I wanted my life to feel. So it took time to figure that out.

About two weeks after that last interview, it was already mid-July. I had been through well over 40 interviews. I realized I didn't want to work for another company unless I was consulting. So, I sent emails to remove myself as a candidate for all the job opportunities that I was in the running for. And instead of applying to my requisite 15 jobs a day, I started building my consulting business website: www.cabralco.com. By the top of August, my site was up and I had no idea what to do next. I hadn't really told anyone what I was doing or what I wanted to do. I was just following my gut and my new guiding message: I can have whatever I want.

I wanted clients.

I was scared.

But I had a feeling things were going to work out just fine.

After chatting with my godparents about it, I decided to take a trip to Italy and Switzerland to clear my mind ahead of what was to come. When I returned, at the end of August, I decided to share that I had opened my consultancy on LinkedIn. I made sure I let my friends and former colleagues know what I was working on as well. By September, I started serious talks with my first client. October brought me another. Throughout the holidays, I had a couple more promising inquiries. So there I was, creating my own invoices and statements of work and negotiating deals for my company! Like, what?! By the end of

January 2018, I had landed enough work to match my Walmart salary. I moved out of my godparents' house in February 2018 a went to DC. By June 2018, I had doubled my Walmart salary. By the end of 2018, I had made over $500,000 in revenue. I was making more than five times my Walmart salary.

On that journey, I literally started to say to myself, every day, "You can have whatever you want. What do you want?" When that felt too hard to answer, I would ask myself, "How do you want your life to feel?" Today, I am still asking myself, and reminding others, "You can have whatever you want" and my life is a reflection of that. Since 2017, I have become a twice-published author. My most recent book, *Say More About That*, was published in 2022 by Wiley. *Allies and Advocates*, my first book, was published by the same publisher in 2020. I have worked with some of the biggest brands in the world, including Amazon, Wells Fargo, Chase, Gap, Inc., and more. My work with organizations has been awarded and I have been recognized in national publications for my expertise. My work has put me on private company planes and sent me to some of the most beautiful international cities – Stabio, Switzerland was a dream! And by the time this book goes to print, I will have had the honor of delivering a TED talk.

My company has made a million dollars or more every year since 2019, even the year I took seven months off after losing a parent. And my wants have not just been professional. Personally, I have gained so much clarity about how I want my life to feel. I live in an apartment that lets me see the sunset every night and offers some of the most stunning views of the city of Atlanta, where I relocated from DC in 2021. I am in a healthy, loving relationship.

I realized and embraced that I did not want to have children. I had spent many years trying to convince myself I did, but that's just what I had been told to want. I now take an annual vacation to my favorite, tiny Caribbean island. I even have friends there now. Life is not just good. It is exactly what

I want. Sure, there are hard times, like losing people, having health issues, and even having the tides turn in friendships. But all that stuff is just life. For the most part, my life now mostly feels how I want it to feel. And I am so, so grateful that I figured out how important it was to start being intentional about what I wanted. If you are anything like I am, you didn't get a lot of encouragement to make decisions about what you wanted for your life. You have had choices, yes – what to have for dinner, what to major in at college, what to watch on television, or which podcasts to pick up. But deciding what you want is about deeply querying things that seem like they are just "how it goes." In my case, that meant asking myself questions like,

Do I actually want a child?

Instead of accepting that having kids is just what I am supposed to do.

Do I actually want to live in that city?

Instead of just going where the jobs took me.

What makes my home feel like home for me?

Instead of wondering if I can just make it work.

How much do I want to make?

Instead of what I think I can make.

Once we are clear about what we want, we can take steps and make decisions that move us in that direction, instead of just accepting what seems available to us. In the same vein, when I consider how I want my life to feel, I make better friendship decisions because I know to query myself if I notice that I don't enjoy how I feel when I'm spending time with someone. Because I know what I want, I make better decisions about who I take on as a client. I even consider what kinds of travel experiences I prefer.

I have more access to equity now because I am not afraid to consider what I want in my decision-making. My overall lived experiences are better. If you, at any point in your life, find yourself looking at your life and not feeling full or joyful about what it is comprised of, consider starting to ask yourself these two powerful questions:

If I can have whatever I want, what do I want?

How do I want my life to feel?

Chapter 11
Love

> "Radical self-love demands that we see ourselves and others in the fullness of our complexities and intersections and that we work to create space for those intersections."
> — Sonya Renee Taylor

Trust your intuition.
Love yourself and others unconditionally.
Let healthy and positive energy be your guidepost.
Establish and honor your boundaries.
Hold gratitude in your heart.

I say these affirmations every day. I know they are cliche, but they resonate with me. If I trust myself, love myself, and move toward the energy I want to give and receive in this world, I will remain on my intended path in life with significantly less strife than I would otherwise. I believe this is true for many people, though I think we each must unpack for ourselves what "loving oneself" means. To find the answer, we must reflect on who we are in the present, and who we want to become. Ask yourself,

> » *What do I want out of life?*
>
> » *What do I need to live a "good life?"*
>
> » *Am I doing things that bring value to my life?*
>
> » *Am I doing things that serve my higher purpose?*
>
> » *What am I moving toward?*
>
> » *Who do I want to be as I move through life?*
>
> » *Who do I want by my side on this journey?*
>
> » *What does love look and feel like for me?*
>
> » *How can I evolve, as a person and/or community member?*
>
> » *Am I embracing patience, purpose, people, presence, and persistence in my life?*

We should reflect on these questions in all areas of our lives, including work, friendship, romance, family, and hobbies. Be as truthful as you can in your answers, otherwise this exercise will not serve you. And that is what we are ultimately moving toward: living and walking a path that allows us to nourish and expand ourselves, to do something more impactful than just "getting through" each day. When we stand in our higher purpose, we can meaningfully serve our communities.

After you have worked through the questions above, deepen the exercise: Choose an area of your life to focus on, then ask yourself what "doing things differently" would look like for you in that particular area. What would it look or feel like to rekindle your ambition? Here are a few examples, from different aspects of life, to get you started:

> » *What might love look like if I changed the framework of my relationships?*
>
> » *How would my life or relationships change if I made time and space to work through past trauma?*

> » *If I do not enjoy my career, and it does not provide for me, what need am I filling by working around the clock?*
>
> » *Who benefits from me "pushing through" a bad situation?*
>
> » *If I am always moving, making, or busy, should "slowing down" be my goal? How might I find rest otherwise?*

During this exercise, you'll find that before you even begin to form your initial answers, additional questions will pop-up. When this happens, follow your intuition. Write those questions down, too. Reflect on your answers. When reflecting, recognize that what each of us wants or needs will look, feel, and be different from that of anyone else.

> Let go of judgments you hold against yourself about what you want and need. Let go of judgments you believe others hold against you. Let go of resentment. This is how we free ourselves. And it is how we can begin to love our true selves. It is some of the most important work we can undertake in our lifetime.

This work — learning to love ourselves unconditionally — is healing work. It is ongoing and lifelong. We must learn to love ourselves or we will never be able to love others. I see so many people unhappy in their relationships because they do not take care of, advocate for, or prioritize themselves. But we need to learn to do so to communicate our real desires and fears more clearly. This will make us better communicators, collaborators, and leaders.

As you work through these questions and personal challenges, remember that we can't impose conditions on ourselves to receive self-love. Let me say that again.

> We can't impose conditions on ourselves to receive self-love.

Instead, we should strive to remain open to change, love, and unforeseen possibilities. The trick to doing so is surprisingly simple: Be honest about your wants and needs. Here's what I mean. Every day, we are faced with a never-ending list of decisions concerning our wellbeing. Take each of those decision points and let them become opportunities to practice authenticity. Consider what you need to feel safe and cared for. Then ask for it. Out loud.

Another way to illustrate this point is to talk about what happens when we don't ask for what we want and need. We become inauthentic. Inauthenticity can look like avoiding looking bad even though we *feel* bad. It could also look like sparing someone's feelings with a lie so we don't ruin a conversation or a night out. Small moments of inauthenticity like this breed more of the same. They may seem trivial at first, but they lead to shallow relationships that cannot weather hard times. And they will slowly eat away at the power of our word — at our integrity — from the inside out. If we fall into this behavioral trap, we will find ourselves unhappy in the long run.

The only way we can unearth the deeper layers of our or someone else's truth is by being authentic. We must explore and reflect on what we don't like, what makes us upset, what doesn't work for us… especially if it makes us uncomfortable. This is how we get to the root of our avoidance. We can't fall back on behaviors that cultivate immediate but fleeting emotional safety. Those behaviors include lying, skirting responsibility, avoiding conversations or people, or being passive-aggressive. They also include withholding our truth, or not implementing boundaries with others for fear of how they will react to our doing so (despite that most people receive "no" better than we imagine they will). These behaviors are all false safeties.

We counter false safeties by establishing boundaries. Real boundaries. We have to learn to say *no* and recognize what *no* feels like in our body and psyche. If we do not do this work, if we do not learn to recognize or love our true selves, we will never be able to do so with others. It's not easy to cultivate space in relationships for this level of vulnerability, but it is a necessary undertaking for anyone in a position of power or leadership.

> A leader gives people opportunities to rise to the challenge of upholding boundaries.

I hope that in sharing these lessons with you, we can engage with open minds, share energy, and co-create a new world together. It's time to build something special, something real, for all of us. The world needs you. We love you.

key takeaways

- 🔓 Let go of judgments you hold against yourself about what you want and need. Let go of judgments you believe others hold against you. Let go of resentment. This is how we free ourselves. And it is how we can begin to love our true selves. It is some of the most important work we can undertake in our lifetime.

- 🔓 We can't impose conditions on ourselves to receive self-love.

- 🔓 A leader gives people around them opportunities to rise to the challenge of upholding boundaries.

transformative learning space

Consider what you read in this chapter and the key takeaways listed above. Write down a few ideas about how you can you apply these learning points to your own leadership practice. Include at least one actionable step you will take to unlock your leadership potential.

case study

Embracing Chiaroscuro
by Stephanie Ann Ball

Stephanie Ann Ball is an Opera Singer, Sound Mediation Facilitator, & Executive Presence Consultant

I must have been about eighteen years old when I heard the term *chiaroscuro* for the first time. Back then, I was a brand new music school student. I was learning the ins and outs of what it would take to be a professional classical singer. Everything felt exciting and fun: the shiny possibilities of brightly colored gowns, lavish travel, and of course, exquisite music laid out just for me. What I didn't realize, though, was that the road to becoming a professional opera singer is a winding one that tests your limits. This career path has a way of uncovering all the parts of ourselves that we're afraid to look at and then forces us to figure out how to deal with them. It's a path that changes you, helps you grow, and demonstrates that the only way to make it through life is to learn to love each and every part of yourself.

In classical singing, *chiaroscuro* means light and dark, just as it does in fine art. If you've ever experienced a vocal performance where you felt the intensity of a singer's voice vibrating in your bones and wrapping you up in delicious musical colors at the same time, you know what I mean. If you haven't felt that, I encourage you to find a way to do so because there's nothing in this world like it. We opera singers need both — the forward, bright, pinging lightness that cuts through the orchestra and allows us to be heard alongside the dark, rich warmth of the voice that fills up a music hall and allows us to be felt. If one or the other is missing, or the combination is unbalanced, music will sound beautiful but noticeably incomplete. Paired together, the vibrations of *chiaroscuro* are life-changing. Healing, even.

Fast forward to a time in my musical career when I was a full-grown adult singer with a master's degree, already working in the music industry. I was good, but I was still holding something back and my new voice teacher knew it. I had been training diligently, but my technique was still lacking, and I was still missing the special magic I needed to take my music career to the next level. I had the *chiaro*, and I had the *oscuro*, but I couldn't put them together. Then, a day came when everything shifted for me. It was a day in which I made sound in a way that would become the centerpiece of my performance and singing style, and a beautiful metaphor for my personal growth journey.

That day, I stood in my teacher, Carol Kirkpatrick's, music studio for our regular voice lesson. She challenged me more deeply than she ever had before. I repeated passage after passage of music with the formidable Carol Kirkpatrick stopping me every time until finally she got up unexpectedly and came right up to me. She stood in front of me and looked right into my soul.

"A voice like yours is a big responsibility," she said. "You have to stop being afraid of it."

At the time I didn't know what she meant, but a part of me felt the importance of her words enough that they cracked me wide open. I started sobbing in the middle of my lesson. Once I gathered myself, I started to sing again. With Carol's support — I mean her literal support while she held out her hands so I could brace my body against hers — I dug deeper than I ever had into my singing technique and found the very essence of my voice. I found the truth of my sound, my soul, my *chiaroscuro*.

Carol and I both leaped back. We were so startled by the change in my voice. I had never made a sound that powerful in my life. And I loved it. I felt powerful, like I could pick up a house. From then on, the questions became, *How do I do that again? How can I get GOOD at this?* Had I known that was another "beginning" in my musical journey, I would have taken a few extra moments to savor the goodness of what it felt like to be held inside the honey-coated sound of my voice. But the excitement was just too much.

The years following have been as expansive as they have been humbling. I have since learned that to truly accept your voice and be courageous enough to share it with others, you have to truly accept yourself. Then you need to take it a step further and love yourself with everything you have. That's what helps you get out of your own way and bring all your gifts together to stand in your power. At times, following our passion can seem unrelentingly difficult, but if you stick it out, you'll find it will be equally rewarding for yourself and for everyone lucky enough to experience your gifts.

The fascinating thing about agreeing to go to the depths of yourself to embrace your true power and embark on a journey of self-love is that once you get started, you can't undo it. There's no going back. And what no one will tell you is doing so requires you to get really comfortable being uncomfortable with the parts of yourself that are hidden in the darkness of your *oscuro*. Carl Jung, a Swiss psychologist, pioneered the concept of shadow work. He describes the shadow as the parts of ourselves that we wish to keep hidden from others. In other words, shadow work is coming face to face with all the parts of ourselves that we cannot stand, or can't stand seeing in others because deep down we know they exist within us. And we hate to admit it.

As I think back on all the years since that life-altering lesson, five things stand out as pillars from which I could build, and which helped me lean further into this work.

The first pillar takes *chiaroscuro* literally: By owning our inner shadows we can fully embrace our inner light. Often, we repress these parts of ourselves and refuse to even acknowledge that they exist within us. This might be because we are ashamed of these qualities, or perhaps we fear them. In my past, that manifested as always wanting to be seen as the good girl, the one who pleased everyone and stayed in her place, who was agreeable and easy to work with. That behavior covered a deeply-rooted, aggressive, sacred rage streak that I was afraid to address for a long time. I think this is common for a lot of people. We want to be seen as good and kind so we can receive love and fit in. So we shun our sacred rage and righteous anger for fear of burning down relationships we care about. But, what if the anger we carry was simply the dark side of something gorgeous about ourselves, like righteous anger when we observe an injustice? Or perhaps one has an ocean of compassion within them and rage is simply a signal telling them there is something that must be addressed. This goes for any emotion that we, as a society, like to pretend we don't all possess, including fear, jealousy, sadness, guilt, shame, etc.

Shining a flashlight on what we believe to be an internal shadow can be the fastest way to get to the healing on the other side of it. And that's when the really good stuff begins to happen for us. And even more powerfully, once we call out a part of ourselves we're not so proud of, we can immediately remove that negative charge brought on by shame. Removing shame is a beautiful, courageous act that helps us walk, talk, speak boldly, and bring the fragments of ourselves back together in an aligned way.

This has been a lifelong journey for me, and new shadows sometimes pop up, surprising me all the time. But having the tools to work through them helps me get on with life. Clearing out the shadows has a way of opening us up to more expansion, too. This was the next pillar for me.

On the heels of getting curious about my shadows came a full-blown spiritual awakening and rapid expansion of my gifts. I did not see this coming! For most of my life, I have heard about how beautiful my voice is, and how others felt healed after listening to me. In addition to that, I have a knack for helping others make sense of their internal wiring so they can move through life in a way that feels easy and natural to them.

A few years ago, during the COVID-19 pandemic, I remember sitting in my office thinking about my consulting practice. I was good at my work, but for some reason, I just wasn't feeling it anymore. This was during the pandemic, so helping people improve their executive functioning skills and get more organized felt off. With everything going on in the world at the time, my work felt superficial and meaningless. Conversely, my intuition was on fire since the world had slowed down. I suddenly felt everything all at once, and I could tell when those around me were in deep pain. That's the day that I knew I wanted to help but I wasn't sure how. So, I sat and wrote, like I often do, and thought about all the different ways I've helped people: soothing people with my voice, helping them feel confident in their own life skills, guiding them to open up their own voices, and generally being a calming presence in people's lives. After affirming with a few trusted friends that I was, indeed, good at all these things, I asked the question that would change the course of my career yet again.

What would happen if I put it all together?

At first, I laughed. The notion of putting executive functioning consultations, singing lessons, subconscious reprogramming, and sound therapy all together seemed ridiculous and confusing. Still, I couldn't let the idea go. And more importantly, I felt excited about the absurdity of it all. I felt complete just thinking about it. I wouldn't have to fragment my work anymore and I could show up for my clients with everything I had. Just to make sure I wasn't totally off-base, I ran this idea by a couple of people I trusted. It was met with not just enthusiasm, but as it turned out, people had been waiting for me to do this! And they were thrilled! So off I went, into a flurry of planning, exploring, playing, and studying. I needed to find a comprehensive way of describing what I was going to do and take people on a journey that made sense *and* facilitated a beautiful transformation.

Diving into a pivot like this required me to step up. I had to own what I did in a way that allowed other people to feel the confidence I had in it. If I didn't believe it would work, then surely others would feel that energy, too. I believe this to be true for what anyone is doing, not just those of us with unconventional careers. If you can truly love every bit of yourself and the work you do, you turn into a lighthouse, shining brightly with your magnetic energy. Your light draws other people to you. Have you ever been to a performance where the artist appears on stage and you can feel the energy of the entire room shift? That is what I'm speaking to here. Those artists know what they're about and they can feel it in every cell of their body. That kind of confidence is contagious, and if you're in a position of leadership it is crucial. When you accept your whole self and have the courage to show it to others, you give others permission to do the same. This kind of courage is not without risk. Embracing risk and rejection is the next pillar beneath my foundation.

When we decide to love ourselves fully and share what we're truly about with the world, we start to agitate other people's shadows. Sometimes that agitation is based on their disagreement with us, other times it's more about reminding someone of the ways they aren't showing up for themselves. Either way, it's okay because it isn't about us. Our job is to keep holding the line and be our whole selves even when someone makes it clear they aren't interested in what we have to offer.

For better or worse, I learned how to deal with rejection very early in my life. When I was nine years old, I remember auditioning for a big church musical. I so badly wanted to be the lead, a cute little angel, so I could wear shiny wings and run all over the stage singing the best solos. I did not get the part. It went to someone a little older than me, who in all honesty, was much better suited for it. At first, I was upset.

Eventually, I felt all my feelings and came to terms with the fact that even though I wasn't right for that part, eventually, I would be right for another one.

That's the thing about rejection. It is bound to happen sooner or later. After hearing thousands of *no*s in the course of my career, I've learned to remember that rejection is inevitable. The key to getting through rejection is remembering that it will bring up emotions for us, and that's okay! It's not fun to be rejected by something or someone we really want, but the more we resist the emotions that rejection brings up, the harder we'll feel them down the line. If we give ourselves time and space to feel the emotions somatically, they will lift off us. And we'll feel more peace about it in the long run. Another important piece of dealing with rejection is not taking it to mean something about us personally.

In the opera world, it's common to audition for something and not hear anything back from the company unless you are awarded the contract. Sometimes, you'll get a rejection letter or email, but silence is also pretty normal. The wait used to feel excruciating. I was left to wonder what I did wrong, and I made up all kinds of stories about why I wasn't good enough to be doing this for a living. Eventually, I got sick of the pity party and realized that the rejections probably weren't about me at all. After talking with lots of other singers, and eventually casting directors, I learned just how true that was. Once, I was rejected by a company that I absolutely adored, only to find out that the board was pressuring them to hire singers from a specific college and that they loved me just as much as I loved them. It just wasn't the right fit at the time!

This is true for sales, too. Oftentimes, when someone turns down an offer to work with me, it's simply because they have someone else in mind or it's not a priority for them at the time. And even when it is because they don't want to work with me specifically, that certainly doesn't mean I'm not good at what I do or don't have value… it just simply is. Remembering that has been another amazing tool in my toolkit. It's a fantastic reminder of how important it is to know what you need and desire so you can leave room for it in your life when it does come your way.

Fully owning my needs and wants and making peace with them is the fourth pillar of my journey of cultivating more self-love. It's so easy to move through life wanting what others want for us, or quieting our desires because we feel like we shouldn't have them in the first place. But having the courage to know those parts of us, and admit it, is another path to loving every bit of the magic within us. Not only that, but it helps others know us better! If you've ever needed something from a friend or partner and were left disappointed because you didn't speak up about it (a.k.a. they didn't read your mind), then you know how important this is. Other people cannot meet us where we are if we don't admit where we are to ourselves first. We need to ask ourselves, *when was the last time I got really honest with myself about what my needs and desires are?* I'm talking about the really deep, juicy needs and desires that make us feel safe and serene when they are met. If it's been a while, I encourage you to do so now. Then take it one step further by figuring out how you can do that for yourself. Finding the answers feels good and empowers us. If we can pour positive energy into ourselves, we will start to radiate the joy we build within. That joy is impossible to ignore.

This is when life really starts to get fun, because we will feel, in our bones, what it means to give from a space of overflow and abundance. When we pour positive energy into ourselves, we are letting our body and soul know how much we love them. That creates the kind of energy that makes giving to others effortless. And for the busy leaders reading this, this is essential. People gravitate toward that energy. When you radiate love, people find it easier to love themselves, too, and then pour it right back into us.

Putting all those things together brings me to the fifth pillar: reclamation of power. It's fascinating how we can give our power away to others, little by little, and unintentionally. That's why doing the difficult work of uncovering what we're really about, pouring positive energy into ourselves, and sharing it with others, is necessary. As demanding as the process is, once we get comfortable with it, we feel unstoppable.

Not long ago, I was pushed to my limit as an artist. Three days before a major performance of a long and complicated work, I came down with a nasty case of strep throat. This is every singer's worst nightmare. I had no replacement, so if I didn't get it together, the show would be canceled. So I pulled out all of the tools in my toolkit. I looked into my shadow and worked through all the rage and fear that comes with, "Why me and why now?". I remembered that I was a professional and extremely well-prepared. In the months leading up to the performance, I had worked hard and relentlessly. I faced the possibility of being rejected by the company after this and not being hired back. Then I figured out what I needed. In this case, I needed rest, medicine, a doctor's visit, a humidifier, and tea… Then, I asked for help from the administrative team and emotional support from a dear friend. After all that, I reclaimed my power and found my center again. It wasn't a perfect performance, but it was still incredible. Even I was in awe of some of the sounds that came out of me because I didn't know what I was capable of under moments of so much tension. That was one of the best parts of my journey. It encapsulated that when we really love ourselves, we find out exactly how bright we are in all our *chiaroscuro*, and the whole world benefits from it. We get the pleasure of standing tall in our gifts for the whole world to see. We lift others up in the process. Together we are unstoppable. And that is what I wish for everyone reading this.

Acknowledgments

"It's a blessing to recognize that you can't do it alone. Sharing and opening your life to others is one of the most beautiful and healthy aspects of life."

MC Lyte

I want to express my appreciation to everyone who has been a part of my life's journey. Firstly, I want to thank God for His love, guidance, and support, especially during moments of uncertainty and fear.

I am grateful to my mom and dad for giving me life and raising me to be who I am today. They have been exemplary parents, and I have learned so much from growing up in a large, loving family.

I want to acknowledge my children, Jason and Jessica, and their mother, Melissa. The experiences I've had with them have contributed significantly to my personal growth and self-discovery as an adult, a father, and a man. Through all my shortcomings, my love for them remains unwavering.

My little sister Karen has been a constant source of support, showing me the true meaning of sibling bonds. I also want to thank my four beautiful nieces, Jazmin, Kamrin, Joslyn, and Kaelyn.

I want to thank my dear friends Amber Cabral and Stephanie Ball. Your friendship and support for this project have been crucial. Thank you for your contributions to this project.

I give special thanks to all the authors who collaborated with me. Kaplan Mobray, you encouraged me to see myself as an author, and Kimberly S. Reed urged me to share my experiences with others through speaking engagements and writing. I am grateful for your belief in me.

Christina Vega, my publisher, thank you for pushing me to follow through and become an author. Your trust in me and your guidance have been invaluable. Thank you to Philip "Sharp Skills" Jacobs for introducing me to Christina and providing the support and tools to make this journey possible. Thanks for the encouragement!

Veronica Very, thank you for inspiring me to write a book and encouraging me to share my inspirational leadership journey with the world. Your influence motivated me to put pen to paper and embark on this writing journey. Maurice Sholas, who would have thought that meeting you at a Forty Niners game and your introduction to Veronica would play such a significant role in my writing journey.

To my poco Community, let's continue our purposeful, organic, captivating, and optimistic journey together. I have learned and grown so much, and I appreciate all of you.

Lily Vasquez Brown is a recent graduate of Western Washington University and a pioneer in many ways. They saw my potential to make a significant impact and joined the team early on to help me get started and realize my potential.

I want to thank the organizations I hold dear: Phi Beta Sigma Fraternity, Inc., NABA, Inc., After-School All-Star, We The Village, and the Love Orphanage.

Special thanks to all the readers, including friends, family, coworkers, board members, and the communities of Drexel University, University of Washington, and Western Washington University. I can't forget my accountants and lawyers, who have served as accountability partners.

Debbie Hassan and Frank Padavano, and all my mentors post-college, thank you for your guidance.

Lana Moorer and Lynn Richardson, thank you for believing in my potential. Your support and involvement inspire me to strive for my complete potential daily.

Index

accountability 17, 69, 85

accountable 40, 85, 110

accountant 68, 133

adversity 15, 67, 135

agile approach 97, 97–99, 99

Amazon 17, 55, 158

ambition 11, 30, 47, 66, 80, 104, 121, 148, 162

anxiety, anxious 24, 46–48, 83, 86

Arkansas 16, 17, 155

authentic, authenticity 10, 17, 22, 53, 69, 79, 87, 121-122, 125, 164, 186

Babwani, Bilal 136

Ball, Stephanie Ann 7, 168, 185

Bouchard-Roberts, Conner 98

boundaries, boundary 10, 12, 58, 79, 81, 86, 88, 89, 90, 104, 115, 150, 161, 165, 166

Cabral, Amber 29, 53, 64, 67, 82, 123, 154

communication 16, 58, 89, 101, 104, 106, 109, 113, 121, 127 community 5, 11, 13, 13–15, 14, 15, 23, 36, 41, 56, 56–57, 57, 67, 95, 111, 122, 123, 127, 127–130, 128, 129, 135, 149, 162

corporate America 9, 56, 83, 116, 135

cultivating patience 23, 46, 67, 116, 147, 175

diversity 29, 96, 104, 117, 148

echo chamber 56

emotional parachute 58

empath 68

empathy 23, 67, 116

empowerment 69, 71, 149

entrepreneur, entrepreneurship 37, 56, 68, 74, 186

equity 76, 96, 148, 154, 159, 185

exit strategy 56

fear 21, 22, 23, 24, 25, 26, 27, 28, 30, 33, 34, 42, 43, 56, 80, 82, 83, 84, 86, 101, 102, 122, 125, 134, 137, 165, 171, 176

Five Ps of Personal Development 15, 17, 149, 150, 152

Ford, Debbie 9

gaslighting 110, 111, 117, 118

Hemphill, Prentis 79

hooks, bell 109

imposter syndrome 24, 133

inauthenticity 164

inclusive, inclusivity 114, 116, 117, 129

integrity 111, 132, 138, 148, 164

intentionality 30

internal work 16, 26, 64, 85

intuition 54, 57, 88, 98, 161, 163, 172

Jacobs, Philip "Sharp Skills" 7, 74, 178, 186

journaling 48, 86

Lake Washington 17

Las Vegas 112, 114

leadership 9, 10, 11, 13, 16, 17, 24, 26, 27, 31, 32, 51, 61, 64, 69, 73, 84, 91, 97, 99, 100, 101, 104, 107, 114, 119, 124, 126, 139, 147, 148, 149, 152, 153, 154, 155, 165, 167, 173

listening 9, 13, 15, 25, 28, 48, 99, 101, 102, 104, 106, 109, 110, 112, 113, 114, 115, 116, 117, 118, 124, 130, 143, 172

Lyte, MC 147, 177

Maathai, Wangarī 21

mask 9, 10, 12, 17

Ma, Yo-Yo 121

mentorship 13, 14, 15, 30, 147

microaggressions 115

Minneapolis 17

Mobray, Kaplan 63, 64, 140, 186

oppression 111

patience 15, 22, 23, 27, 45, 46, 47, 48, 50, 150, 162

Perel, Esther 95

Peréz, Krista 96

persistence 15, 162

perspective 24, 25, 28, 55, 66, 70, 99, 112, 113, 114, 117, 134, 143, 151

Philadelphia 11, 13, 17, 55, 56

poco (restaurant) 23, 24, 25, 28, 29, 47, 48, 56, 57, 58, 109, 127, 129, 130, 133, 136

practice 23, 35, 41, 42, 45, 46, 47, 50, 54, 64, 70, 86, 96, 110, 118, 122, 164, 172

present, presence 10, 15, 16, 27, 36, 48, 54, 56, 58, 59, 63, 64, 68, 69, 84, 86, 87, 88, 89, 100, 101, 106, 110, 111, 115, 118, 131, 135, 148, 150, 162, 172

privilege 66

purpose 15, 29, 45, 57, 59, 65, 68, 72, 80, 89, 90, 102, 116, 123, 140, 141, 142, 143, 144, 150, 154, 162

reactive culture 98

Rosario, Sam 136

Schweitzer, Albert 53

Seattle 15, 17, 23, 25, 55, 56, 186

self-actualization, self-actualized 114, 131, 137

self-awareness 26, 31, 122

self-belief 42, 55

self-examination 79, 86, 87

self-flagellation 136

self-healing 81, 136

self-love 79, 161, 164, 166, 170, 175

self-reflection 10, 54, 82, 84, 86, 90, 123, 131

self-satisfying needs 30

Smith, Will 131

social media 122

strategizing 22

Taylor, Sonya Renee 161

transparency 68

trust 16, 17, 27, 28, 47, 48, 56, 69, 87, 88, 95, 96, 97, 98, 99, 100, 101, 102, 104, 105, 106, 111, 118, 122, 124, 150, 151, 161

Trust Model 17, 102, 106, 124

truth 9, 11, 17, 22, 25, 38, 41, 65, 70, 79, 95, 98, 121, 123, 125, 151, 164, 169

Vega, Christina 7, 33, 178, 187

Virgo 9

vulnerability 25, 54, 70, 87, 122, 150, 151, 165

Walmart 16, 17, 154, 155, 158

workplace 16, 29, 47, 48, 76, 96, 97, 99, 100, 105, 109, 114, 115
　culture 47, 48, 96, 97, 100, 105, 114
　norms 48
workplace dynamics 99

About the Author

Jesse Rhodes Jr. is an experienced thought leader, philanthropist, and entrepreneur with over 25 years of professional experience, including positions at Amazon, Deloitte, Ernst & Young, Target, and Walmart. Mr. Rhodes also serves on several boards, including the Chair of After-School All-Stars' Puget Sound Chapter, Vice-Chair of the Board of Governors of Columbia Tower Club, and has also been serving as the National Director of NABA, Inc., of which he holds lifetime membership since chartering the student chapter at his alma mater, Drexel University, in 1994. Jesse also chartered Drexel University/Univ. of Penn undergraduate chapter, remains a proud member of Phi Beta Sigma Fraternity, Inc., conducts extensive humanitarian work with Love Orphanage in Haiti in partnership with We The Village Organization, and also volunteers with several organizations, including Wonder of Women International, which focuses on serving Black women and girls, among others.

About the Contributors

Stephanie Ann Ball

Stephanie Ann Ball, lyric coloratura soprano, is swiftly taking her place in the world of classical music with her warm, strong, lyric voice. As a highly sought after concert artist and curator, she has performed on stages alongside world-renowned composers such as the award-winning Mark Hayes, and the Craig Bohmler, the composer of the highly acclaimed new opera, *Riders of The Purple Sage*. Ms. Ball has been invited to perform as a guest artist on concert series across the country including St. Peter's Cathedral in Mansfield, OH, the Cathedral Basilica of the Immaculate Conception in Denver, CO, and has commanded the stage of the famous Red Rocks Amphitheater in Colorado as a soloist for the Colorado Council of Churches.

Amber Cabral

TED and keynote speaker, author, inclusion consultant, and podcast host Amber Cabral is the founder and CEO of Cabral Co, an equity and inclusion strategy firm. She chairs Brown Girls Do Ballet and has authored two books, *Allies and Advocates*, (Wiley, 2020) and

Say More About That, (Wiley, July 2022). Amber is best known for delivering respectful, authentic, and no-nonsense training, strategies, and content rich with simple but impactful steps and eye-opening insights that inspire change. Originally from Detroit, Michigan, Amber currently resides in Atlanta, Georgia. She is visibly passionate about improving representation, education, access, and opportunity for underrepresented and marginalized people.

Philip "Sharp Skills" Jacobs

Philip "Sharp Skills" Jacobs has been called a modern-day renaissance man. He is an entrepreneur, award-winning hip-hop artist, speaker, author, senior consultant, and inventor. He was the first Executive Director of Washington Employers for Racial Equity (WERE), a coalition of 80+ companies in Washington State committed to making the region equitable for Black Washingtonians and all people of color. Philip is a distinguished alum of Seattle Pacific University, where he obtained a bachelor's degree in business administration. He holds the PMP credential in project management, is the author of *The Elephant in the Room* and *Accuracy*. He has independently produced numerous music albums. His proudest accomplishment is being the father of Philip Jr. and Jonathan. Philip is from Inglewood, California, and now calls Washington home.

Kaplan Mobray

Recognized by *Meetings and Conventions Magazine* as one of the nation's top business speakers, Kaplan Mobray is one of the world's most dynamic and inspirational business speakers and award-winning author of *The 10Ks of Personal Branding*. Wharton educated, he has been featured on CNN, FOX, Businessweek, The Wall Street Journal, and shares his message to NFL players and fans annually at the Super Bowl. He continues to serve as a consultant to fortune 500 companies working with business leaders to elevate Performance,

Excellence, Branding, Leadership Effectiveness, Innovation, Diversity Equity and Inclusion and Workforce Transformation. Kaplan has delivered presentations in 23 countries across 5 continents. All of his innovative presentations have been described as life-changing events. In his personal pursuits, Kaplan is a professional saxophone player. Kaplan resides in West Nyack, NY and is active in civic and charitable organizations.

Christina Vega

Christina Vega (they/them) is the publisher at Blue Cactus Press, where they make books that offer liberatory approaches to being in better relationship to ourselves, our communities, and the earth. At Blue Cactus Press, Chris makes books alongside other industry professionals from historically marginalized groups. Chris is also a Queer Chicana poet from the borderlands of Texas & New Mexico. They live on Puyallup and Nisqually Land. They published their sophomore poetry collection, *Vega*, in 2023 through Blue Cactus Press. Chris believes we have the power to reshape our communities with principles of Emergent Strategy, transformative justice, and collective laboring of love. They believe revolution starts at home.